Praise for
Scoring in the Red Zone

"Leaders aren't born; they are made. In *Scoring in the Red Zone*, Spencer offers his blueprint for leadership under pressure, based on three core concepts and seven operating principles. It's great stuff! Touchdown, Tillman!"

—Rick Warren

Author, *The Purpose Driven Life*

"In *Scoring in the Red Zone*, Spencer Tillman uses this football analogy to create a book that is must reading for leaders in all stations of influence."

—Ken Blanchard

Coauthor, *The One-Minute Manager®* and *The Secret*

"Highly inspiring and spirited, *Scoring in the Red Zone* will meet the needs of thousands of leaders seeking a proven leadership solution for these challenging times. From the minute I read the introduction I knew Spencer Tillman had something important to say. What followed did not disappoint."

—Clark Hunt

Chairman, Kansas City Chiefs

"*Scoring in the Red Zone* resonates relevancy. Spencer Tillman's three core concepts and seven can't-miss operating principles will go a long way in helping leaders restore lost trust."

—John McDonough

Former Vice Chairman and CEO,
Newell Rubbermaid
Current Chairman, McDonough
Medical Products Corporation

"*Scoring in the Red Zone* is a must-read for everyone interested in understanding the anatomy of ethical leadership. This kind of leadership is needed in order to win in the twenty-first century."

—Kirbyjon H. Caldwell
Pastor, Windsor Village United
Methodist Church

"Heartwarming, invigorating! We need more of this. Spencer Tillman has shown us that the most effective leadership is cause-driven. *Scoring in the Red Zone* is excellent in its variety and depth."

—Woody Johnson
Chairman & CEO, New York Jets

"When Spencer Tillman took stock of his life and said, 'Business as usual will no longer cut it; I have to do things His way,' it resonated with me. *Scoring in the Red Zone* means that you pray, you prepare, you trust, and you act according to God's purpose for your life. Now that's a game plan!"

—Ernie Johnson Jr.
Emmy Award Winner & Studio
Host, Turner Sports

SPENCER TILLMAN is a sports broadcaster, former NFL player, journalist, businessman, churchgoer, devoted husband, and father of four daughters. He has written pieces for the *Wall Street Journal*, the *San Francisco Chronicle*, the *Houston Chronicle*, and others. An all-American running back for the University of Oklahoma, he started and ended his pro career with the Houston Oilers and in between played with the San Francisco 49ers, where he won a Super Bowl and served as team captain. In 1999, Tillman joined CBS Sports for *College Football Today* as well as to cover NCAA Men's Basketball.

SCORING IN THE RED ZONE
How to Lead Successfully When the Pressure Is On

Spencer Tillman

NELSON BOOKS
A Division of Thomas Nelson Publishers
Since 1798

www.thomasnelson.com

Published in Nashville, Tennessee, by Thomas Nelson, Inc.

Nelson Books titles may be purchased in bulk for educational, business, fund-raising, or sales promotional use. For information, please e-mail SpecialMarkets@ThomasNelson.com.

Tillman, Spencer.
    Scoring in the red zone : how to lead successfully when the pressure is on / Spencer Tillman.
      p. cm.
    Includes bibliographical references and index.
    ISBN 0-7852-0558-6 (hardcover : alk. paper)
    1. Leadership. 2. Success. 3. Pressure. I. Title.
HD57.7.T53 2005
658.4'092—dc22   2005015658

Printed in the United States of America

05 06 07 08 09 QW 5 4 3 2 1

To my mother
La Rue Helen Tillman
1935–2002

A son couldn't have had a better mother.
I consider it the highest of earthly honors to have been your son.
Thanks for the wisdom you and Dad deposited in me.

CONTENTS

Introduction: A Marathon Walk with God   ix

1. What Is the Red Zone?   1

2. What Does It Mean to Score?   13

3. Crucible Experiences   31

4. Core Values   49

5. Visioning   67

6. Harnessing the Will   85

7. Establishing Traction   101

8. Creating Connectivity   115

9. Finding Focus   131

10. Igniting Passion   147

11. Striking a Balance   161

12. Beating the Clock   177

    Conclusion: Final Thoughts   195

    About the Author   201

    Acknowledgments   203

    Notes   207

INTRODUCTION
A Marathon Walk with God

When the man who was about to end my mother's life entered her hospital room on January 23, 2002, the thirty people crammed around her bedside fell silent. All we could hear was the rhythmic wheezing of the respirator as it kept what was left of LaRue Helen Tillman alive. Mother, wife, missionary, friend of rich and poor alike, but now there was nothing left of her but an empty vessel, a shell.

After checking my mother's vital signs one last time, the white-clad respiratory therapist turned to face us: my older sister, Sharon; my younger sister, Bettina; my brother, Anthony, the eldest; my father, Jack Tillman Jr.; and me. "I know you've already discussed this with the doctors," he said, "and I realize your mother expressed her wishes clearly before she slipped into a coma. But I need to ask you one more time: Are you certain you want to go ahead with this?"

One by one, we all acknowledged that he should proceed. Of course, none of us wanted to see him end my mother's life. For years, we had stood alongside my mother as she fought against diabetes, which had systematically cut her down. But when she was struck by two heart attacks within two days, the fight seemed to go out of all of us. All we wanted now was to make her final days as comfortable as possible.

When I flew in to Tulsa earlier that night from Houston, my mother pulled me close to the bed, hugged and kissed me, then looked into my eyes. "I'm tired, son," she said. At that moment, I realized it was over. My mother just didn't talk like that. She was a strong woman, a fighter. But she had met her match. I went ahead and canceled all of my commitments for the foreseeable future and prepared to accept what we had all seen coming but hoped would never happen. Now, less than twenty-four hours later, it was about to end once and for all.

Without any further discussion or ceremony, the man in the white uniform put his hand on the ventilator tube and pulled it out of my mother's mouth. The moment the tube came out of her mouth, her eyes opened wide, and she let out a cough. After that brief, involuntary spark of life, my mother lapsed back into her former comatose state. When the respiratory therapist left, we all began to sing, quietly at first. Passing nurses looked on in wonder and bewilderment as we lifted up praises to God even as our mother lay dying. With each passing song, the time between my mother's breaths grew longer and longer. We knew she had finally breathed her last when the room was suddenly pierced by that all-too-familiar sound—the steady, sixty-cycle hum of a heart monitor that has suddenly become a redundant piece of equipment. It was a sad moment, but it was also a peaceful one, a quiet end to sixty-seven years in the service of her Lord.

As I went through the motions of those next few days, I could not escape some nagging questions about my life. Here I was, a former NFL player who had been the captain of a Super Bowl team; a successful sports broadcaster for CBS—one of the few African-American men to reach such a level—a businessman, jetting around the country making deals; and a husband and father of four beautiful girls. I had a good life, a great life in comparison to most. And yet, something was missing, something right at the core of my being.

I thought about my mother. Although she had a happy home life growing up, her parents were not people of means. But my mother did not allow that to hold her back. She picked cotton in Arkansas as a child to earn money and worked her way through college against incredible odds. From there, she went to work as a missionary, both at home and abroad, sharing God's love with thousands of people.

I was amazed at the crowd who turned out for her funeral, not only at the number of people but also the different walks of life they represented. I saw everyone from mayoral candidates and state representatives to street people. Obviously my mother's life had meant something to each one of them. I wondered about my own funeral. Would there be the same sort of turnout for me?

Then I remembered how my mother used to pray for her family, to the point where she often fell asleep kneeling beside her bed. Stalwart and strong, my mother had always been in our corner, teaching us the right way to live. And yet beyond her determination I knew was a will even stronger than hers. Something she had taught me throughout my youth was that I might chart my own course in life, but I was by no means the engineer of my existence. My will acted within the larger context of the will of God. If I was to achieve the objectives He had laid out for me, I had to align my will with His. I knew this lesson well. And yet, like so many other people, I had failed to apply it systematically to my life. Yes, I had success, but it came at a price.

My broadcast and football careers had left little time for my family. Speaking engagements, spiritual and volunteer commitments, and business deals cut that slice of time even thinner. I had achieved many things. But did my life even hold a candle to what God had envisioned for me? Had I even fulfilled half of my potential? As I considered my mother's example, I began to have my doubts. She had been given so little, but she had turned it into something extraordinary. In contrast, I had been given a fortune. But did the return on that investment even compare to what she had gained from hers?

Thoughts like these nagged me for the next two months. Then early one March morning, I was sitting in my home office, thinking and praying, as I am in the habit of doing at the start of each day. Suddenly, I felt an impulse to get up and go for a walk. Having no idea where I was headed or why, I simply obeyed.

Outside, it was a crisp, clear morning. For no real reason, I headed toward the perimeter of our subdivision, which was located on the outskirts of Houston. Once I left our subdivision, I continued until I reached an intersection between two major highways, and I turned left. Suddenly, I felt my entire countenance change. Despite the fact that I was now walking along a busy freeway, a sense of peace came over me, and I began to hear from God. At first, it was just little bullets of information or insights relative to picking up the gauntlet and making the most of my time on earth. There was no structure to it. But I sensed something special was going on, because I did not normally have such thoughts in my head.

At this point, I had walked for about seventeen miles, and I still had no idea where I was going. As I walked, I began to notice trains going in and out of the nearby Sugar Land sugar mill. The mill had stood there since the late 1800s. Every day since then, trains had been hauling sugar, water, and other supplies to and from the mill. Thus, it was not uncommon for traffic to be backed up along this stretch of highway as the vehicles waited for trains to clear the crossing. This day was no different.

As I approached the railway crossing, still receiving these random messages from God, I began to ask myself what I was going to do with all of this information. How was I going to incorporate it into my life? Then the story of Jesus' parents traveling home from the Passover came to mind. I recalled how His parents were a day into their journey before they even noticed their son was missing. After a frantic search among their friends and relatives, they raced back to Jerusalem in search of Jesus. Three long days later, they found Him in the temple courts where He was putting the religious teachers through their paces. When Mary confronted her son about His absence and how worried He had made her and Joseph, Jesus simply replied, "Why were you searching for me? Didn't you know I had to be in my Father's house?" (Luke 2:49 NIV).

Suddenly, God showed me how this story was an analogy for my own life. Jesus had always been with me on my journey, had always enjoyed at least a token role in my existence. But at some point along the way, I had inadvertently left Him behind. Like Jesus' parents, I was well into my travels before I even realized something was wrong. It hurt me to think that it had taken so long for me to notice His absence. If I had been living in intimate relationship with Jesus, the loss of His presence should have signaled an immediate void in my life. But I had continued right on ticking. I had reached a level in my career where my abilities and my relationships afforded me all sorts of opportunities. In the eyes of many people, I had "made it." And I prided myself in being able to wheel and deal with the best of them. Pray about this business deal? Why bother? All the pieces are here, and it's clearly a great opportunity. Don't worry; I can pull it off. I know the score. If Jesus was not behind those deals, I should have noticed His absence at the bargaining table. But I didn't.

A healthy form of anxiety constantly plagues a person of purpose; a need to be moving constantly toward some purpose or end. That description summarized me to a tee. The problem was, while the God-given desire to achieve was still the driving force of my life, the goals upon which I had set my sights were anything but God-ordained. I had drifted off course. The things I had been pursuing were not wrong, necessarily: business deals that promised to make a lot of money for everyone involved; volunteer work with the Juvenile Diabetes Research Foundation and other organizations. They were all "worthy causes." But how many of these activities were derived directly from the purpose for which God had placed me, Spencer Tillman, on earth? As I pondered this, I heard a familiar voice continually murmuring in the background: "Anything born of the flesh will end in the flesh . . ."

So if Jesus was not present and active in my life, where was He? Where had I left Him behind? Mary and Joseph found Jesus in the temple. He was spending time with His Father, doing things that were connected with His purpose, preparing for His future ministry. When was the last time I was in a space, like Jesus, where the Father could teach and direct me? How long had it been since I lingered in my Father's house so that He could show me His vision for my life? I did not want to think about it. For too long, I had forsaken God's guidance and determined my own direction in life, only asking for His blessing after the verdict had been determined or seeking His help when things went wrong. It reminded me of Proverbs 14:12: "There is a way that seems right to a man, but in the end it leads to death" (NIV). My path had not lead to death—at least not yet. However, it was quickly racking up an abundance of anxiety, fear, and uncertainty.

God started talking to me about these issues as well. But He didn't just leave me hanging there in confusion and despair. He offered me a glimmer of hope; He showed me a way out. I will share more about precisely how He did that later. For now, suffice it to say that, realizing I had finally received the message God wanted to share with me during this interlude, I turned quickly toward home, my mind reeling with new ideas.

When I entered our house, I went straight into my home office. For the next few hours, I pored over my Bible, the Internet, and any other source of information that would help me flesh out the ideas churning in my mind. Everything was coming to me in real time: ideas for books, an interactive CD, speaking engagements, you name it. Throughout all of this, God was making one thing abundantly clear: He was calling me to be a leader. Having been called to leadership all my life, that should have been a no-brainer. However, God also insisted that "business as usual" would no longer cut it; I had to do things His way. No more being Mr. Dealmaker and flying all over the place. God wanted me to spend time with Him, learning what He had called and equipped me to do; not what I had called and equipped myself to do.

I also sensed that this call to leadership was not for me alone. I was to share it with my family, my peers, and with the nation at large. I felt a special burden for other African-Americans. Due to God's grace, I had managed to rise to a level in my career that, regrettably, few African-Americans achieve. Thus, I felt a duty to be an example to those who would follow me, to make the most of all I had been given.

At the end of the day, I sat back in my chair and shook my head in wonder. Little did I realize when I had awakened that morning all that God had prepared for me that day. I had started out dissatisfied with my life, worrying about the future, and unable to see a way out of my circumstances. But God had lifted me out of my chair, transported me a total of twenty-six miles—a distance equal to a marathon—then brought me home with a fully realized vision of what He wanted me to direct my energies toward for the foreseeable future. It was a remarkable day, a day that is still bearing much fruit, the least of which is the book you now hold in your hands. I pray that the principles contained herein will equip and inspire you as much as they have me.

1

WHAT IS THE RED ZONE?
The Ultimate Place of Testing

Trailing by a field goal and backed up on their own 8-yard line with just over three minutes left on the clock in Super Bowl XXIII, San Francisco 49er quarterback Joe Montana glanced over at the sidelines during a television time-out.

"Hey, H, isn't that John Candy in the stands, next to the exit ramp?" Montana was talking to Harris Barton, his starting right tackle. Harris was known for keeping a perpetual scowl on his face even in the most non-threatening of circumstances. This moment was no exception. I can understand H's frustration. How could Montana be thinking about anything other than the desperate reality of the 49ers' situation? He should have been focused on how he was going to get them out of this mess, not checking the stands to see who was going to watch him do it. After all, this was sports' biggest stage, and it looked like the 49ers were about to flub their lines big-time.

Despite H's concerns, the play sequence that followed was the stuff of which legends are made. As quickly as Montana identified the late comedian John Candy chatting, he switched his persona and redirected his focus to the task at hand. "Okay, let's do this." Over the next three minutes, Montana, a surgeon in shoulder pads, proceeded to dissect the Cincinnati Bengal defense. He led his offense on a ninety-two-yard sortie that ended with a winning touchdown toss—a vectored laser shot to John Taylor that passed right between the outstretched hands of two pawing Bengal defenders—with only thirty-four seconds left on the clock. It was a tremendous drive. And yet he made it look like a simple outpatient procedure.

The orchestrator of many great come-from-behind wins during his career, Joe Montana had an ease on the field that defied the pressures imposed on him during such high-stakes moments. His consistency in producing results forged what some have called the "49er mystique." Players knew that as long as number 16 was in the huddle, their chances of winning had just gone up substantially, and they carried themselves accordingly. Though I wasn't yet on his team, I could not help but be affected by Montana's prescience as I watched that game. Over a thousand miles away, my second NFL season complete, I sat back in my anchor's chair at KPRC-TV in Houston and thought, *That's where I want to be.* Not just playing in the Super Bowl but competing shoulder to shoulder with this particular team. There was something special about Montana, to be sure, but there was also something uncommon about the entire organization.

I had heard from friends around the league that wide receiver Jerry Rice and running back Roger Craig ran the length of the field in practice after every catch or carry. Not content to make it an offensive drill only, cornerback Ronnie Lott and defensive back Dave Waymer would often be in close tow, mirroring Rice's and Craig's every move defensively. Great players like these guys did not require big crowds to put forth their best efforts. Their compulsion came from within, and that is what put greatness within their reach. They knew the improvement process was perpetual and without boundaries. And I knew that watching high-profile leaders preparing in this focused way could be the catalyst that made average players good and good players great. I would do anything to become part of that roster.

As fate would have it, soon afterward I became a free agent, opening the door for me to move on to any team in the league. I wrote the 49ers specifically. Less than a week later, I was on a plane, talking to their people. Two days after that, I became a 49er. My dream had become a reality. Now I just had to prove that I belonged there.

The Red Zone: A Definition

Players like Joe Montana were particularly brilliant when it came to scoring in the Red Zone. The Red Zone is that fiercely defended piece of turf from the 20-yard line to the goal line at either end of the field. It's called the Red Zone because once you enter that area, it is tremendously difficult to score. The color red signifies danger, emergency, to pull out all the stops. The reasons for this designation are many.

With the size of the field reduced to a mere 1,300 square yards (from a total size of 6,500 square yards), the defense has less area to defend and can concentrate its efforts on the line. Likewise, the offensive team has less room in which to maneuver, thus limiting the number and type of plays they can execute. You can expect to be hit sooner and more violently in the Red Zone, because the defending team is also making what amounts to its last stand on a given scoring drive—if not the game—so their resistance will be particularly fierce. Finally, as is the case throughout the game, the clock is always winding down toward 00:00.

Up against such formidable obstacles, scoring in the Red Zone requires every player to execute his assigned task in a precise and timely manner. The cost of mistakes in the Red Zone is particularly high. Coaches and players will confirm that nothing kills a team's confidence faster than a turnover or a sustained drive that produces no points, especially if that drive ends in the Red Zone. No one wants to come away from the Red Zone empty-handed. Teams with the highest scoring percentages in the Red Zone win more games than their opponents.

So even before you enter the Red Zone, you must devise a solid game plan, including plays designed specifically to maximize your strengths and exploit the opposition's weaknesses.

Red Zones Exist Both on and off the Field

On the football field, the Red Zone is not so much a location as a situation—a set of circumstances that, taken together, put an enormous amount of pressure on both the individual and the team to do their jobs right. But Red Zone situations aren't restricted to the world of sports. We encounter them in virtually every area of life—at home, at school, at work, at church, in our marriages, and in our community.

Take work, for example. Your boss has just informed you that a project you thought you had weeks to complete is due tomorrow. And if you don't hand it in on time, a lucrative account may be lost. You know that if you fail, your job could be on the line as well. Fighting to quell a sense of rising panic, you toss everything aside and rush out to assemble your team. But then you discover even more bad news: one of your key players is at home sick. Now the rest of you will have to not only pull off the impossible, but you'll have to do it while being one man short. You have definitely entered a Red Zone.

In football, what you need to do to pull off a win is obvious: get the ball across the goal line, kick a field goal, or at least get another first down so you can set up a new series of plays. But real life is rarely so black and white. Think about marriage, for instance, a prime setting for many Red Zone situations. You and your spouse have just had an argument over finances—again. You made an investment that has suddenly gone sour. Your spouse didn't want you to do it, but, because you "had a feeling," you went ahead and invested the money anyway. Now, not only are you out the money, you're on the outs with your spouse. Reconciliation is the goal. But where is the goal line? And how will you know when you've crossed it? It is unlikely a man in a black and white striped shirt will be there to throw his arms up in the air when you've done it—even though sometimes you probably wish there was! The aim of this book is to help you and your team develop exactly that—a solid game plan so you will be able to operate in the Red Zone with aplomb.

How to Know When You Are Entering Condition Red

To help you recognize when you are entering a Red Zone, I have created the following litmus test. You know you're entering a Red Zone when: (1) the need to achieve your *objective(s)* is suddenly increasing at the same time that (2) the *obstacles* between you and your objective(s) are growing more formidable, (3) your options for overcoming those obstacles are decreasing, and (4) time is running out.

Now let's unpack this definition.

Your Objective

In this regard, there are a number of questions you can ask: What is your objective? How will you know when it is time to spike the ball and do a little dance in the end zone? Is there a deadline to meet? A product to create? A teenager to discipline? Make sure you and your team are clear on this from the outset. Otherwise, your Red Zone experience will turn into a rout as you all run different and often conflicting patterns when the ball is snapped.

Your objective should always contain both qualitative and quantitative components. We often get hung up on hard data and measurable results. Like a football team, all we want to do is put points up on the board. But life is about a lot more than simply moving the ball down the field, unlike how it is in sports. How we play the game of life really is as important as whether we win or lose. Unlike us, God is more concerned with our spiritual development than fulfilling our personal wish lists. God has no problem with us prospering materially or relationally, but not at the expense of our souls or character. So make sure you define your objective qualitatively as well as quantitatively. That is, in addition to stating what you would like to achieve, also describe what kind of person or team you want to become as a result of the experience.

Another main question in regard to your objective is, what is at stake? In most Red Zone situations, the stakes are heightened considerably. Your ability to score in such situations will generally decide whether or not you win the game. In football, defenders do not give up yardage or points easily. They will try to punish you every step of the way. So if you have made it this far, you had better make it count, because you do not know when or if you will get another chance. Life is full of similar "make it or break it" opportunities. The opposition is fierce. You are competing for a job or a contract. You are racing for a deadline. If you fail to convert, everything you have been working toward could be lost—your career, your marriage, or your ministry.

The Obstacles

Once your objective is established, you must consider the obstacles you will face along the way. These come in two types: visible and invisible. In football, the most obvious visible obstacle is the other team. Other visible obstacles include the crowd, injured players, and the weather. Examples of visible obstacles in the world of work include rival organizations, an unpleasant boss, and lack of finances.

The invisible obstacles you face at work are similar to those encountered in football: i.e., fear, inexperience, and conflict. Another major invisible obstacle is a value conflict. This is when your core values conflict with those of another individual or organization. Such conflicts form the heart of Red Zone situations, because the outcomes of these conflicts determine the kind of person you become.

Fastin's Dilemma

Let's take a brief look at how this works:

Micah Fastin is senior financial vice president of a Fortune 100 high-tech corporation. One day, Fastin is called into CFO Alexander Harding's office. It turns out the sales department has booked millions in revenue to an off–balance sheet partnership of the corporation but inadvertently failed to report a crucial detail to finance—a side letter allowing their client the option of full reimbursement and full cancellation without cause and with no penalties. The impact of the side letter, should the client opt to invoke its terms, would be a 60 percent reversal in revenues.

Harding asks Fastin to find revenue—and quickly—to protect their projections in the event of a cancellation. Fastin responds with an obvious solution: restate the revenue and liability, take the hit, and get it over with. Harding, however, refuses in an uncharacteristically belligerent manner. This leads Fastin to suspect there is more to the story than Harding is letting on. Indeed, what Fastin does not know is that the restatement will sink the possibility of an acquisition CEO Jeff Scanning has been negotiating for months.

Regardless, Fastin knows that if the SEC and Wall Street find out they have not restated, it will open the entire organization to liability and an almost-certain stock crash. The board meeting is in three hours. What should Fastin do?

This would be quite a dilemma for some. But for the individual who is committed to scoring in the Red Zone, the choice, although difficult, should be crystal clear.

Not all Red Zones are the same. To help differentiate between different levels of real-life Red Zone situations like the one above, I have created a four-level scoring system. After you read the descriptions of each level, try to figure out how you would rate Fastin's situation.

- *Level one:* This is a Red Zone situation where you are tempted to compromise your core values "when no one else is watching." Examples of level one Red Zone scenarios include being tempted to cheat on your income tax returns or including false credentials on your résumé. In each situation, you can probably get away with your behavior, but you will pay a price from a character point of view.

- *Level two:* This Red Zone situation is where your core values conflict directly with an individual with whom you have an established relationship—your spouse, your child, your boss, etc. Here, the potential for conflict and lingering ill feelings is far greater. A good example of a level two Red Zone situation involving family is a young couple whose values and lifestyle choices conflict with those of their parents.

- *Level three:* At this stage, your moral conflict moves from the personal to the organizational. A person may still represent the organization, but the consequences of your decision will have a drastic and immediate effect on your relationship to the group as a whole. The most common type of a level-three Red Zone situation is where you are asked to "sell out" your values for money, to do something that is morally questionable and possibly even illegal.

- *Level four:* The most complex and challenging type of Red Zone situation is when your core values conflict with society at large. This was the situation faced by prophets such as Isaiah and Jeremiah in the Bible. At the time, kings wanted prophets who would applaud their decisions and actions, not question them. Dissenting prophets like these two men were often imprisoned or killed if they did not jump into line. The same thing happened to Jesus when He dared to stand up to the corrupt religious culture of His day. Modern-day prophets or dissenting voices like Martin Luther King Jr. and Gandhi have faced similar fates.

The Call to Rebuild a City

Throughout history, the Jewish nation has known the dark day and the dreary night. It should be no surprise then that circa 1000 BC, Israel found itself split into two regions: the Northern and Southern Kingdoms. The Southern Kingdom's capital was Judah, which some years later became the epicenter of history's greatest collective endeavor to restore a fallen city—Jerusalem. Generations since have pointed to this time and to the effort demonstrated as their motivation to reclaim what had been given to them graciously by God. And, as is often the case, they also vowed never to return to the ways that caused them to lose hold of God's gift in the first place.

Some additional context may be helpful in grasping the widespread uncertainty of the times. The Babylonians, who previously conquered Jerusalem in 597 and 587 BC, were themselves overthrown by the Persians a few years later. Ultimately, Cyrus, the king of Persia, permitted many of the Jews who had been exiled to Babylon to return to their homeland. The number that repopulated the city and surrounding area is believed to be between forty and fifty thousand. Upon their arrival, they attempted to restore all semblances of their previous lives, including the reconstruction of the temple, the center of their religious activities. Their restoration effort gained new momentum after yet another setback—a series of attacks by the Samaritans—but the temple was eventually completed. By then, Ahasuerus, aka Artaxerxes I, was in charge of Persia. Like Darius and Cyrus before him, Artaxerxes showed tremendous compassion toward the Jewish people and their religious practices. Even so, while the restoration of the temple represented an impressive engineering accomplishment, it was still only a shell. Several leaders and prophets—including Haggai and Zechariah—attempted to reinvigorate the Jewish people in their rebuilding efforts. However, they only managed to achieve marginal results.

Ezra, another great leader, took up the baton and continued to lift the spirits of a once-proud people who, although few in number, in many ways remained imprisoned in Persia. History is often a long and tragic illustration that pathologies such as poverty, low self-esteem, broken homes, etc., produced by systemic slavery do not die easily. Indeed, they often linger for generations as those who enjoy privilege—and, thus, are in the best position to effect change—struggle against the notion of extending rights and privileges to the oppressed, especially if that means giving up some rights and privileges of their own. Such was the case in Persia.

Enter Nehemiah circa 445 BC. Nehemiah was a thousand miles away from Jerusalem, serving as cupbearer to King Artaxerxes in the city of Susa, when his brother Hanani arrived with devastating news: "Those who survived the exile and are back in the province are in great trouble and disgrace. The wall of Jerusalem is broken down, and its gates have been burned with fire" (Nehemiah 1:3 NIV).

Let us not be fooled by Nehemiah's title as cupbearer. He was far more than a butler. Only the most trusted individual was chosen to taste food to be eaten by Artaxerxes. He was capable of and charged with much more than his title suggested. He was Artaxerxes's right-hand man. Upon hearing the news of Jerusalem's destruction, Nehemiah's knees buckled, leaving him in a heap of mourning humanity. Even as he wept and prayed, however, the seeds of a vision to restore Jerusalem were being sown.

In his quest to rebuild the walls of Jerusalem and, subsequently, her people, Nehemiah faced every level of Red Zone situation, from situations where he was tempted to compromise his principles in private to outright threats on his life. Throughout every stage of reconstruction, Nehemiah was accosted by Tobiah, Geshem, and Sanballat, three "locals" who were not very excited about the rebirth of the Jewish nation. This treacherous trio tried everything from ridicule to innuendo to intimidation in their efforts to halt the reconstruction process. They accused Nehemiah of wanting to rebuild Jerusalem just so he could proclaim himself king.

When they realized they could not tarnish Nehemiah's reputation with their lies, they sent a false prophet to warn Nehemiah that his life was in danger and to recommend that he take refuge in the temple. But Nehemiah was not one to hide from trouble. More importantly, he was not in the habit of relying on his "own understanding," as Proverbs 3:5 describes human wisdom. Instead, he relied on the Word of God. Thus, Nehemiah knew that it was unlawful for anyone other than the high priest or the Levites to hang out in the temple. Obviously, hiding out in the temple would discredit his leadership, so it was a no-brainer that this "word" did not come from God. Instead of obeying the false prophet,

Nehemiah asked God to remember this trio who had worked so hard to derail God's plans to restore His city.

In addition to these personal challenges, Nehemiah was also hard-pressed on many other fronts, such as limited manpower, limited funds, and the sheer enormity of the task. But Nehemiah was able to overcome these challenges largely by applying the concepts and principles described in this book. The times may have been vastly different from our own, but the temptations and challenges Nehemiah faced are no different from the ones you face as a leader over two thousand years later. Thus, his life is an excellent and relevant model of leadership for the twenty-first century.

A Shrinking List of Options

In football, passing the ball in the Red Zone is a risky proposition because it is extremely difficult for receivers to get open when everyone is crowded into such a small area. Your safest bet is to stick with your running game—if you have one, that is! But sometimes you just have to improvise. The same is true in life. When the crunch hits, many times you do not have the luxury of doing things the way you would like to do them if conditions were ideal. So you have to do the best with what you have.

This is exactly what Nehemiah did when he realized he did not have enough men to defend the city and construct Jerusalem's walls. After taking stock of his situation, he came up with an innovative if not ideal solution: have the men work with a trowel in one hand and a sword in the other. That way they would always be poised to build or defend, whichever was the most compelling need at a given moment. Nehemiah also had his men sleep at their posts rather than return to their families at night. That way the city had round-the-clock protection. It was not a fun situation for anyone, but it did not last forever and it got the job done. And that's what matters most.

The Time Factor

By the time you reach the Red Zone in football, you have two sets of downs at best to reach your objective. But if the defense is on their game, it is unlikely you will even get through one set before they shut you down. So time is restricted, and you have to make the most of every precious moment you are given. In this sense, life can be characterized as one big Red Zone. There is never quite enough time to do the things you want to do or to do them the way you'd like them done. But in the Red Zone, it's as if the clock speeds up even more.

So Where Does This Book Fit In?

Your strategy for scoring in the Red Zone can be divided into two phases: preparation and execution. In the preparation phase, the first thing you need to do is determine your objective and what is at stake. This is where the three core concepts—crucible experiences, established core values, and visioning—I describe in Chapters 3, 4, and 5, respectively, come in. Once you know where you would like to go, the next step is to assess your ability to get there. This includes assessing the strengths and weaknesses of your team as well as those of your opposition. Based on the information you have gathered, you can create a winning strategy that plays to your strengths and exploits the opposition's weaknesses.

Now you're ready to put your plan into action. This is where you begin to practice the seven operating principles I describe later on in this book: harnessing the will, establishing traction, connectivity, finding focus, passion, balance and distribution, and proper use of time.

When it comes to both the preparation and execution phases of leadership, I would also like to draw your attention to the positive spiritual resources you can draw on to make your Red Zone strategy a success. Thus, I share the following two principles when it comes to the execution phase of your Red Zone attack:

No relationship, no protection. As a leader, you need to imagine yourself as the quarterback and God as your offensive coordinator. Situated high above the fray, with all of the obstacles and opportunities in clear view, He is in the best position to see what needs to be done. However, if you are not in contact with Him, there is no way you can benefit from this perspective. Consequently, as team quarterback your job is to consult with God first and then run the plays He calls, not call your own shots.

Trust your coach. It is not enough to say, "Yes, coach," every time God tells you to do something. You have to lace up your cleats, jog out onto the field, and do it! But such instinctive obedience can only come out of a trusting relationship. As you approach each Red Zone experience, be assured that God has never reneged on a promise or obligation. God has made some incredible promises to us in the Bible, all of which are premised on our obedience. If you are acting out of obedience to God, you can enter every Red Zone with the assurance that He will help you pull off a win.

Becoming an effective leader isn't just about doing the right things; it's about becoming the right kind of person, preparing yourself for battle before you ever step onto the field. For that reason, this process begins with discovering and recognizing your core values and then bringing them in line with God's objectives. This first step is crucial, because by aligning your convictions with God, you are aligning your character with the ultimate model of integrity. Ironically, however, it's often not until you enter a Red Zone or "crucible experience" that your true core values are exposed. By then, it is usually too late to do anything to change them, at least as far as that particular Red Zone is concerned. But you can always apply the lesson learned later on.

Once you are on solid ground from a character standpoint—backed up by a solid history of integrity—it is time to start birthing a vision. Here's where the seven operating principles come into play. Mastering them is what will turn you into a playmaker, enabling you to execute any plan no matter what kind of Red Zone you are in. Whether you are facing a crisis in your family, business, church, community, or any combination of the above, your ability to score in the Red Zone is guaranteed when you use God's playbook.

2

WHAT DOES IT MEAN TO SCORE?

Defining Success in an Age Defined by Change

Defining what it means to score on the football field is simple. On a team level, it means winning the game, the division, the conference championship, or the Super Bowl. On an individual player level, it includes scoring a touchdown or a sack, breaking a team or league record, or being chosen for the Pro Bowl. Once you move away from the football field, however, defining success becomes increasingly difficult.

Defined by Core Values

For one thing, we all define success according to our own specific set of core values, which may be stated or unstated (more on core values in Chapter 4). For example, if one of our core values is acquiring wealth, we will determine our level of success according to the amount of money in our bank account. In addition to wealth, other common measures of success include power, status, happiness, popularity, or our "win versus loss record." The fact that we define success according to our core values is not a bad thing. However, because we all hold to a different set of core values, it is difficult for us to agree on what success really is. And it is also difficult to determine if the values we are using to define success are the correct ones.

Qualitative and Quantitative

A second factor that makes success so difficult to define is that success has both a qualitative and a quantitative dimension. Happiness, popularity, status—these are all qualitative measures of success. They are intangible, meaning our perception of how we score in these areas is entirely subjective. Wealth, position, and our win versus loss record are quantitative gauges of success. That means we can measure them objectively by calculating our net worth, checking the nameplate on our office door, or tallying up the number of goals we have achieved versus those we have not.

However, what happens if you meet all of your goals in a year but break every rule in the book to do it? Are you successful? Or what about if everyone knows your name but you cannot afford to put food on the table for your family? Are you successful? On one level, yes. On another level . . . once again, the qualitative and quantitative aspects of success collide, making it difficult to offer a definitive description of that term.

A Moving Target

To put it in football terminology, the "chains" of success keep moving. For example, just because you score a first down does not mean you can stop and rest. You still have to go out there and score another, and another until you reach the end zone. Then you have to go out there and do it again and again until the game is over. The same is true in life. Each accomplishment does not win you the game; it just moves the chains farther down the field. And the process does not stop until the game—your life or your career—is over. You will exhaust yourself if you think there is nothing more to life than moving the chains. Success is more than just a string of achievements. We live in a "wired/tired/expired" world. What is deemed successful today is old news by tomorrow—if not by midnight. The targets are constantly moving, faster than ever before. Trying to keep up is like trying to score a first down but having no idea how many yards you need to gain in order to do it.

The Pace Factor

Another factor that makes success difficult to define is the ever-increasing pace of change in society. This rapid change is driven by a number of causes.

Moore's Law

In 1965, Gordon Moore, cofounder of Intel, observed that the number of transistors per square inch on integrated circuits (or "chips") had doubled every twelve months since the integrated circuit was invented. Moore predicted this trend would continue for the foreseeable future. In subsequent years, the pace slowed down somewhat. Nevertheless, data density has continued to double every eighteen to twenty-four months. This trend has been dubbed "Moore's Law." Most experts expect Moore's Law to hold for at least another ten years.

But Moore's Law is not just driving advances in technology. It is also setting the pace for virtually every other sector in society. Rapid change and improvement has come to be expected in every product, from vehicles to breakfast cereal. Do we really need all of this innovation? Probably not. But once we start down that road, it is very difficult to stop. Perhaps computing power will hit a wall in ten years; perhaps not. But you can rest assured we will have built up enough momentum by then as a society that it will be virtually impossible to slow down. We are addicted to change— the faster the better. We demand it. And corporations are more than happy to give it to us. Because each time they bring out a new product, it means more dollars in their pockets.

A "Get Rich Quick" Mentality

Perhaps at no time in our history have so many people been so focused on attaining "the good life." Ironically, at no time in the past four decades has the good life been so difficult for the average person to obtain. These dreams are fueled by a number of factors, including the "dot-com" feeding frenzy of the late 1990s, our obsession with highly paid athletes and celebrities, and the prevalence of lotteries with obscenely high cash payouts. These factors and others contribute to a prevailing mythology that the good life is possible. Forget about going through the long process of carefully managing, saving, and investing our money wisely as our parents did. All we have to do is invest in the right "hot" stock, buy a winning lottery ticket, sign up for another credit card, or come up with—as author Michael Lewis calls it—the "new new thing."[1] Few people think about the actual cost of an item anymore. All they want to know is what the monthly payment will be—never mind that financing a car, a home entertainment system, or a vacation means they will wind up paying far more than the asking price. We do not want to wait for the good life. We want it now.

Another major factor contributing to this mentality is advertising. To keep up with quarterly earnings expectations, corporations have to keep selling new products. Playing to our negative felt needs, they present these new products—cars, vacations, boats, and so forth—as the solution to our unhappiness. They are pitched as "givens." They are considered luxuries that anyone with a steady job can afford. The message is, "What we're selling is within everyone's reach." And if it isn't, there's always that financing option . . .

This sophisticated media apparatus does not just influence our decisions. It also adds to our frustration, because the truth is, the relatively simple, repetitive abilities required to do certain jobs no longer command the inflated and secure salaries they did in the 1950s, 1960s, and 1970s. Subsequently, the masses are no longer assured of attaining the good life anymore simply by doing unskilled labor for a large corporation. Their jobs pay less and, in the worst cases, have disappeared altogether. Some people have been able to find work in other areas, take on second or even third jobs, or improve their earning potential through education; others have not. Nevertheless, they keep on trying, because until they get these things, they do not feel successful. That's because so many of us place our identities not in who we are but in what we buy.

Increased Competition

The rules of business are changing constantly, forcing all participants into Red Zone scenarios with increasing frequency. One of the key drivers of this change is increased competition. Coming to terms with the effects of this ratcheted-up culture and the reasons behind it gives us a chance to anticipate change and respond appropriately.

In 2003, Microsoft tried to buy the online search engine, Google, for $10 billion. Stop and think about that figure for a moment. Do you think Microsoft believes owning the leading Internet search engine is important? You better believe it. The problem is, Google founders Larry Page and Sergey Brin refused to sell. So what do you think the fellows at Microsoft's Internet Research and Development department are up to right now? That's right: figuring out a way to beat Google at its own game. As Netscape learned, when Microsoft sets its sights on you, your days are numbered. Let's just hope Google does not have to learn that lesson as well.

But it is not just Microsoft that Google has to watch out for. Hard on Google's heels are Alltheweb.com; Inktomi.com (who was purchased by Overture Services in 2004); and a number of other search engines, all vying for top spot. What all of this means is, in today's economy—whether you are a business or an individual—being on top today offers no assurance that you will remain in that position tomorrow. Someone is always nipping at your heels, so there is the constant, unrelenting pressure to innovate, improve, and change your product or service. It never stops, and it never slows down. Sometimes I wonder how people like Bill Gates get any sleep.

Shareholder Expectations

A CEO's fortunes ride on the price of his or her company's stock. With more people investing in the stock market than ever before—many of them with no idea of what they are doing—stocks have become increasingly volatile. The pressure on corporations to hit quarterly and annual targets has never been more intense, because if they don't, people will put their money elsewhere. The effect of this demand forces corporations to focus more and more on short-term profits rather than the long-term viability of the organization. And if CEOs and other executives cannot meet investor expectations legally, there is always the "cooked books" option. I do not have to mention the litany of executives who have succumbed to this temptation over the past few years.

Rapid Change and Scoring in the Red Zone?

Change is happening faster than ever before. In many cases, technologies, business models, and marketing techniques are becoming redundant almost as fast as they emerge onto the scene. This rapid change has an enormously detrimental effect on your ability to score in the Red Zone. Here are a few reasons why.

Short-term vs. Long-term Thinking

Like CEOs, the average person is also tending to focus on short-term gains rather than long-term financial viability. It has never been easier to get credit. Coincidentally, over the past few years, we keep setting new records for personal bankruptcies in America. In the twelve months leading up to June 30, 2004, for example, more than 1.6 million Americans filed personal bankruptcy petitions. That is an increase of 9.6 percent over the previous year, which was also a record breaker.[2] And, like corporate executives, average people are also tempted to cut corners when times get tight as they strive to gain a more favorable lot in life. According to a recent survey conducted by the IRS, the number of people who believe it is okay to cheat "a little here and there" on their income taxes has gone up by 50 percent.[3] No matter what your definition of success may be, I am willing to bet that going broke or going to jail is not part of it.

An Increasingly Short "Rise and Fall" Cycle

Think about movies. Do you remember a time when studios would begin a film's release in large centers, like New York and Los Angeles, and then continue to roll it out over a few months across the rest of the country, counting on a word-of-mouth snowball effect to make it a success? Starting with *Jaws*, all of that changed. Instead of a slow build, studios realized they could recover their costs and start earning a profit far quicker if they released films simultaneously on as many screens as possible. Today, A-list films are released on over three thousand screens across the country, and they often make it or break it according to their opening weekend box office numbers. Theatrical runs are shorter than ever, and the DVD is released less than six months later.

How about publishing? Depending on whom you talk to, approximately fifty thousand books are published in the United States each year. Despite the proliferation of big chains like Borders and Barnes & Noble, shelf space is increasingly difficult to come by. If you want your book displayed in a prominent position, you have to pay dearly for the exposure. Even then, publishers usually give a book only one to two weeks to catch on—if they put any marketing money behind it at all. If it's a hit, they will throw more money at it. If not, it's on to the next book. Unless an author is extremely fortunate, the big break he or she has been working toward all of his or her life may be over in a matter of days, leaving that writer *dazed*.

One more example of the rapid pace of change, this time from the world of football: Jerry Glanville, my former coach at the Houston Oilers, once quipped, "The NFL really stands for 'Not for Long.'" He was correct. Players that are talented and fortunate enough to make it and want to extend their careers past the 3.4-year average had better adapt or risk extinction. As with most businesses, the NFL is a machine that never stops running. Like it or not, players are really nothing more than interchangeable parts. This became clear to me personally in 1992 when I called George Seifert, head coach of the 49ers, to declare my intention to return to the Houston Oilers (later to become the Tennessee Titans). Even though I had played several years with the 49ers, it took them all of seventeen hours to fill my roster spot. I was impressed with my replacement but not nearly as much as the swiftness with which they acted.

What is true of the entertainment or sports industries is true for most spheres of business today. The time we are given to prove ourselves is getting shorter and shorter. We either adjust to the new work order or risk being replaced. We either move up or move out of the way. More frequent downsizings, capsizings, and "rightsizings" are forcing business owners to squeeze out more profits and increase shareholder value regardless of who has to pay for it. Such cost-cutting actions contribute, in part, to why the average worker today will be employed by as many as ten different organizations by the time he or she reaches retirement age. I do not need to tell you that the "gold pin" era of labor—one dedicated worker + one loyal employer = gold pin and retirement—is a thing of the past.

Stress and Burnout

With so much uncertainty at work and in the culture at large, it is no surprise that a growing number of people are experiencing higher levels of frustration, depression, stress, and burnout. According to a stress awareness publication put out by the National Institute for Occupational Safety and Health (NIOSH), 29–40 percent of workers often feel stressed or burned out by their work.[4] This stress is carrying over into the home, turning what should be a haven into an emotional dumping ground where overworked, dysfunctional people unload on one another, adding to rather than countering their families' feelings of uncertainty about how to achieve success in life.

After considering all of the above, the question begs: With so much uncertainty, why are we still clinging to outmoded definitions of success, such as wealth or status? We simply have to redefine what a successful life really is. Otherwise we run the risk of becoming a nation of clinically depressed underachievers. But how do we do this?

Redefining Success

As Rudyard Kipling said in his classic poem "If," "If you can keep your head when all about you are losing theirs and blaming it on you . . . You'll be a man, my son." Change is all around us. It is not slowing down, and it is not going away anytime soon. You need to be aware of it, and you need to learn how to deal with it. But you cannot allow it to distract you from your prime directive, which is serving God. Circumstances change, but God does not. Thus, when we talk about success, the definition is no different today than it was ten or ten thousand years ago. It is still based on the following two core values: (1) loving God and (2) loving others. We know these are important values to God, because when Christ was asked to name the two greatest commandments, this is exactly how He responded:

One of them, an expert in the law, tested [Jesus] with this question: "Teacher, which is the greatest commandment in the Law?" Jesus replied: "'Love the Lord your God with all your heart and with all your soul and with all your mind.' This is the first and greatest commandment. And the second is like it: 'Love your neighbor as yourself.' All the Law and the Prophets hang on these two commandments." (Matthew 22:35–40 NIV)

Part of loving God means learning about Him and His character and how He desires to mold you in His image. One of the best ways to learn about God is by reading the Bible (more on this in Chapter 7, "Establishing Traction"). The Bible contains scores of examples of people just like you and me—some who succeeded and some who did not. We can learn much from them, particularly the reasons behind their successes and failures.

If you are having trouble deciding whether or not to pursue a certain goal, all you have to do is hold it up against these two core values—love of God and love of neighbor—and the answer should become clear. Will this goal bring you closer to God? Is it in line with His character, His teachings, and His principles as we read them in the Bible? How will this action affect others? Will it harm them or help them? Are you merely pursuing the goal for your own selfish gain, or are you honestly seeking the good of the entire group?

Make Relationships a Priority

We have a saying in Texas that goes like this: "faith, family, and football." The first two items are certainly more important than the third, but the point is made. Faith and family come before everything else. Yes, even before your job. To paraphrase the words of Christ, "What good will it be for a man if he gains the whole world, yet forfeits the souls of his children?" (Matthew 16:26). When we talk about men providing for their families, we immediately think of food, clothing, shelter—the basics. However, provision also includes spiritual instruction. Focus your attention on raising children who love God, who have the ability to discover their own unique purpose in life. Your investment in this sort of human capital is the wisest investment you will ever make.

Family should never be sacrificed in the pursuit of success. It is true that from the moment Adam and Eve sinned, God gave man the responsibility of being the primary breadwinner. In Genesis 3:19, God speaks these words to Adam: "By the sweat of your brow you will eat your food until you return to the ground, since from it you were taken; for dust you are and to dust you will return" (NIV) Most men do not have a problem with the notion of working hard to provide for their families. Usually, we commit the opposite sin: working so hard that we marginalize our wives and children. I have heard all the arguments for and against working long hours. And I have been grossly guilty of working too much myself at times. I used to brag about the fact that I had never missed a day of work for any reason in my twenty-plus years of professional work. Then it dawned on me that my diligence had caused me to miss out on so many opportunities to influence my children by tucking them in and praying with them at night.

I know it is not always practical—and I definitely do not want to dump more guilt on you—but you can and must be there for your family. There are times when it is necessary to work long hours, such as when you are starting a new enterprise or your work requires travel. However, let us not forget the words of a mechanic who had a full day's work at the shop. Later that evening, a coworker saw him playing catch with his son. Surprised that he still had any energy left after an exhausting day, he inquired, "Mike, aren't you tired?"

Mike nodded. "Yes, nearly spent."

"Then why are you out here running around playing ball?"

The wise father answered instantly: "I'd much rather have a backache tonight than a heartache later on."

Mike knew something millions of men should know but too often choose to ignore. Children don't learn through osmosis. They need examples, images, and concrete representations of how their lives should be lived. And the best person to provide that sort of thing is you.

The good news is, God's definition of success will never become irrelevant, and it is not subject to market forces. Because of this immutable plumb line, you can get a reliable read at any time on where you stand relative to God's definition of success. And here's even better news: not only is God's definition of success attainable; it is guaranteed if you embrace His vision. That's because "we know that in all things God works for the good of those who love him" (Romans 8:28 NIV). The culturally defined descriptions of success I described at the beginning of this chapter are often by-products of true success, but they should never be mistaken for the genuine article.

It is not just family that is at risk if you fail to order your life correctly. Strong, dependable friendships are today more challenging than ever to establish and nurture. Everyone is so busy; it is becoming increasingly difficult to connect with others. That doesn't mean friendship has diminished in importance. In fact, it is more important than ever. So do not let your friends slip down the list of priorities as you decide how to carve up your diminishing slice of free time.

Realize That Success Is a Journey as Well as a Destination

This goes back to what I said earlier about qualitative versus quantitative measures of success. Reaching our goals is important, but not at any cost. When it comes to success, never sacrifice quality for quantity.

Keys to Scoring

Every football coach has a list of favorite plays for getting the ball into the end zone. Here are my favorite strategies when it comes to scoring in other areas of life.

Choose the Right Goals

As I have already attempted to make clear, one of the first keys to scoring is having your priorities straight. That means choosing goals that are based on your core values.

Second, your goals must be specific. State your goals using verbs that clearly communicate the purpose of the objective and very little else. It is one thing to say you are going to be the best football team in the league. It is an entirely different thing to say you are going to win the Super Bowl. One goal is general. The other is specific, and it lends itself immediately to a detailed game plan.

Next, goals should be measurable. If you do not know where you are in respect to your goal, how will you ever know when you get there? Going back to that quest for the Super Bowl, you can easily measure your progress by keeping an eye on your win/loss record versus that of the other teams you are up against in your division, conference, or the league as a whole.

Fourth, goals must be agreed upon by the team. This is called "buy-in," a concept I talk about more in Chapter 4. Do you have advocates within the organization who want to see you succeed? Have they bought into your vision of success?

Fifth, your goals must be realistic. This does not imply that it will be easy to achieve. On the contrary, they will require you and those laboring with you to stretch your skills, but not beyond their limit. For example, a team that sets its sights on a Super Bowl championship but suddenly finds itself with a 1–5 record after six games is all but assured of missing the goal. However, if a recovery is at all realistic, the best possible situation exists to motivate the participants. Desperate players make for dangerous competition. Opponents, beware!

Finally, your list of goals should include both long- and short-term objectives. Realistic time limits must be applied to each goal so you know how to budget your time and so that everyone on the team will have a growing sense of excitement and anticipation as the deadline draws near. Most people perform best under this type of positive pressure. We will discuss more about goal setting in Chapter 5, "Visioning."

Pray

This one is pretty obvious, but the list would not be complete without it. In Chapter 7, "Establishing Traction," I explore what happens when we pray. Once you discover the series of events that are set in motion when you spend some time on your knees, you will change your mind about prayer being nothing but a routine salutary practice as we part company or prepare to eat or sleep. As for Nehemiah, it will become your central empowerment device. As we will learn later, prayer was the secret weapon behind Nehemiah's effort to complete one of the most important reconstruction efforts in the history of Jerusalem while simultaneously protecting the city from attack. You can put this same weapon to work for you as well.

Position Yourself

The true pace at which success occurs is a delicate balance of God's timing, your abilities, and your readiness to take advantage of opportunities as they come along.

Look for a Golden Opportunity

I first got to know Steve Young when he was a frustrated, curly-haired kid, whom I nicknamed "Bobby Brady." At that time, Steve was fresh off two difficult experiments with the Tampa Bay Buccaneers and the USFL's Los Angeles Express. Then the 49ers made him backup quarterback to the legendary Joe Montana. Unfortunately, while Steve's address had changed, now he was in an even less likely position to actually play. So, from 1987 to 1990, Steve stewed on the bench in frustration while Joe added to his legend.

Steve's fortunes changed radically a short time later, however, when, during a nondescript play at training camp, Joe tore some ligaments on the inside elbow of his throwing arm. Just like that, Joe's season was over before it even began.

This unpredictable occurrence opened the door for Steve to step in and do his stuff, setting off the mother of all quarterback controversies when Joe returned a year later. In the end, Joe left to help Kansas City take their franchise to the next level before he retired after the 1994 season. Steve, of course, went on to build his own legend. None of this would have happened but for circumstances beyond Steve's control. But when Steve's number came up, he was ready. Like Steve, you also need to get busy doing what you can so when the opportunity presents itself, you are *positioned* to take full advantage of it.

Commit to Constant Improvement

When trades are made and salary caps reached, assumptions are made concerning players and their relative abilities and personal habits. Any quality scout can look at game tape and evaluate what kind of athlete a guy is. However, of equal interest these days are a player's character and work ethic. A cornerback, for instance, who is fully committed to total, year-round readiness, is more than just a good player. His impact on younger players is incalculable. In effect, he becomes an example that coaches point to in a time when attitudes of entitlement seem to be pervasive. Therefore, he has more value. You can increase your value in the same way by committing yourself to constantly improving your "game," whatever that happens to be.

Don't Wait for an Invitation to Innovate

Success involves moving forward even when outside motivation is lacking. The NFL is a unique example of this, because, unlike most enterprises, it is shielded from direct competition. No other football "company" is out there successfully challenging the NFL brand. Despite the NFL's competitive advantage, the protectors of the NFL take very little for granted. The league is constantly evolving and improving its brand. It even launched its own television network in 2003. This was a brilliant preemptive maneuver to show the broadcast entities that the NFL was positioning itself as an enterprise with options for when their television contracts come up for renegotiation.

You can apply this corporate mind-set to your own life. Personal positioning means more options; and more options generally lead to more success and a greater perceived value. The NFL could have reclined on its competitive advantage and waited to see what the market would bear. But the people at the NFL's helm were not satisfied with that. They wanted more. In the same way, if you have talents, skills, and qualities on which an employer places value, protect them and improve them, and you will be in constant demand. But do not wait for an invitation to do this. Do it now.

Don't Resist Change; Adapt to It

Significant numbers of people remain ill equipped to take full advantage of the opportunities afforded by the technology-fueled, new world order. In the old large-scale production era, jobs were repetitive, seldom changed, and, most importantly, they were secure. Things are much different today. In these times of extreme competition, constant improvement and adaptation are a must. Individuals and organizations that do not embrace this reality will be trampled by the herds that rush to accept the challenge.

In football, if a coach in the college or NFL ranks cannot turn things around in three years or less, he is shown the door. There is no such thing as a five-year plan anymore. College athletic directors, like their professional counterparts—NFL general managers—are running businesses that are subject to the same market forces as any other enterprise. They must innovate and create new and more robust revenue streams to remain competitive, or they risk conceding ground to competing institutions.

The smart teams have adjusted. Athletic directors are no longer former coaches or once-great players who have worked their way up the ranks. Today, college athletic directors are skillful marketers and managers, not stoic relics who smile, play golf, and beg alumni for money. They are sophisticated strategists with big visions and the savvy to bring them to fruition.

Reactions to Change

Studies have shown that people generally pass through eight stages when confronted with change. We will examine them briefly here.

Shock: This is similar to what happens when you hear about a sudden death. You do not really do much at this stage, but rather try to come to terms with what the new situation entails.

Denial: Overwhelmed with grief, fear, or shock, at this point you simply try to close your eyes to reality, stick your head in the sand, and pretend the change is not really happening. Not the healthiest place to be, but we all pass through this stage at one time or another.

Loss: This is where the grieving begins. Finally, you are able to recognize the gravity of the situation, and you begin to mourn the loss of the old ways and your identity within the old system.

Confusion/Disorientation: Also part of the grief process, this is when you find yourself in a no-man's land between the old world and the new one, and you don't know which direction to go. Do you cling to the old, or press on with the new?

Anger: At this point, you have decided to actively resist the change, even sabotage it if you can. You pull into a shell of self-preservation, stifling creativity and innovation. Like a child resisting his or her parent, you plant your feet in the ground and refuse to move forward. Sometimes, you even seek to recruit others to your position. This is a crucial stage, because how you handle it will basically make or break your future. At this point, you will decide to either move forward with the organization in the hope of undoing "the damage," as you see it, or leave the organization altogether.

Passive Acceptance: If you choose to stick with the organization, sooner or later your anger will melt away into a form of passive albeit grudging acceptance of the new ways. You'll come to your senses and realize the old ways are gone indeed. A new way of doing things has come, so you might as well get on with it.

Exploration: Once you overcome your initial resistance to the change, you may actually become quite excited by the new options and opportunities the change has created. You will begin to explore these options as you seek to find a place for yourself in this new world.

True Acceptance: At this point, you embrace the change, realizing that change is a catalyst for continual improvement, not an obstacle to be resisted or overcome.

With so much change happening so often and so quickly, everyone has the potential to get hung up at one stage or another. In fact, change is happening so quickly that you may still find yourself in a state of shock over one innovation, only to be bombarded with another! The key to getting through this process is to recognize that change is the norm, and your reactions to it—both positive and negative—are natural and to be expected. At all stages of the game, your goal should be to embrace the change and find a way to make it serve you rather than hinder you. Keep that attitude, and you can't go wrong.

Don't Let the Crowd Throw You Off

Whether you are on the football field or in the boardroom, you live your life before a crowd. However, the size of the crowd watching you should have zero bearing on how hard you work. This is one of the axioms of Christian preparedness. True believers do everything as unto the Lord. That means you should exhibit the same passion, persistence, and perseverance whether you are in front of ten people or one million. That's because when you think about it, ours is always an audience of one: God. When aspiring broadcasters, sports agents, and young businesspeople ask me for advice about how to get started, I tell them to do what I did: go somewhere and do something. All that matters is that it is aligned with what you want to do ultimately. If the audience count becomes a significant factor early on, that is not a good sign. Anyone whose essence is wrapped up in the amount of attention he or she receives as a result of his or her exploits is in an extremely vulnerable position. When I played football, we used to call such players "junkies"—attention junkies.

In the end, success—your ability to score in the Red Zone—will always be measured according to God's terms. And you can rest assured that because He has a vested interest in your success, He will never walk away from you when the going gets tough. Authentic success as God spells it out is attainable and measurable. However, if you insist on holding fast to culturally prescribed definitions of success to determine whether or not you have arrived, success will remain precarious, elusive, and unpredictable, diluting or derailing your ability to live a full life.

3

CRUCIBLE EXPERIENCES
The Necessary Storms Before the Calm

Now that you are up to speed on what the Red Zone is and what it means
to score, it is time to start looking at the three core concepts and the seven
operating principles that will help you get through the Red Zone and into
the end zone. We will discuss the core concepts first, the first of which is
crucible experiences.

Crucible Experiences: A Definition

Simply put, a crucible is a transformational experience that produces fundamental changes in the way you view life and your place in it. Almost any
experience can qualify as a crucible—a birth, a death, a new relationship,
a new job, or a change in location—as long as it brings about this paradigm
shift. Even though the word *crucible* seems to imply negativity, an event
does not have to be a tragedy before it qualifies as a crucible. What trans-
forms an ordinary experience into a crucible experience is how you
respond to it. As long as the event causes you to reformulate your sense of
identity and/or your purpose in life, it qualifies as a crucible. The death of
a loved one, something all of us go through at one time or another, is a
good example of a negative crucible experience. Landing a job, inheriting
money, or winning the Super Bowl are all examples of positive crucible
experiences. Each one of these experiences can have a transformational
effect if you allow that to happen.

Leadership expert Warren G. Bennis calls such experiences "crucibles" after the graphite or porcelain vessels medieval alchemists utilized in their efforts to transform nonprecious metals into gold. The chief value of crucibles in this context was their ability to withstand extreme heat, making them ideal for the refinement process. For our purposes, however, it is not enough to merely endure the extreme heat that a crucible experience can produce. The individual who is transmuted by a crucible must emerge able to construct and articulate a narrative that logically expresses how the experience will direct his or her future activities. Alchemists failed to turn ordinary metals into gold. But if you want to score in the Red Zone, you cannot afford to follow in their footsteps.

Crucibles Aren't Just Additive—They're Transformational

Crucible experiences do not just add to your knowledge of life; they permanently alter your perception of the world in which your life is lived out. Crucible experiences change the way you think, the way you treat others, the way you conduct your business, and the way you spend your resources. These changes are not temporary. They represent a permanent shift in the way you think and act. In my case, as I describe in the Introduction to this book, the death of my mother caused me to go through a significant paradigm shift regarding the goals toward which I was striving, the methods I used to get there, and the motives that drove me. That's fundamental change. I am certain you have had similar experiences.

Crucible Experiences Reveal Core Values

The primary value of crucible experiences rests in their ability to unveil our core values, for better or for worse. They are like checkups or self-tests that help us determine what our core values are and how strongly we adhere to them. This is vital for leaders to know, because, as you will discover in the next chapter, these values form the bedrock of a leader's character. Without character, it is impossible to lead successfully, at least over the long term.

Character Unveiled

As naturally as a duck takes to water, we are drawn into deceit by our desires. If we think having a certain thing will enhance our status, acceptance, or happiness, we will do almost anything to get it. Such strong desires often expose core values that do not reflect emblematic character. This can be a good thing or a bad thing, depending on what we do with what we discover. I suspect most of us can recall an occasion during our formative years that caused us to feel "less than" or just plain jealous of others because of something they had and we did not. Such feelings can bring out the worst in us, as it did with me when I was eleven years old.

I played baseball before I participated in any other organized sport. Our team was part of the Salvation Army league. We practiced and played at a place in north Tulsa called the Maybee Center. All of the basic equipment required to play the game was provided, and I had my own fielding glove. However, most of the other players had one extra piece of equipment that I did not: a batting glove. I would describe my desire to own one as nothing less than insatiable. Not having a batting glove did not prevent me from playing baseball, and playing it well. Without a glove, however, I did not "look the part." Functionality and style: Sounds like a tag line for a luxury SUV commercial. But it is a poor excuse for stealing a batting glove. Alas, that is exactly what I attempted to do.

When I arrived at the store, I made a beeline toward the sports section. There it was, in a case protected by a silver sliding lock: a Wilson batting glove. An attendant opened the door for me, and I slid the first glove off the rod hanger. Then the attendant locked the door and disappeared several aisles down. I handled the glove for a moment, imagining all that it would do for my burgeoning baseball "career," then transferred it to my left hand while I reached into my right pocket to retrieve my money. This is an important detail: my mother had given me enough money to purchase the glove. Still, for some reason, I put the glove in my pocket and began to exit the store. Suddenly, that same attendant who had helped me before appeared at the end of the aisle and asked me what I had done with the glove. An indescribable chill came over me as I had been caught red-handed. I was silent as he walked me back to the security office, where I hemorrhaged tears in isolation and in silence as I waited for my mother to pick me up.

As I look back on that dark day, I recall thinking about only two things as I sat there in that lonely K-Mart office: the embarrassment to my parents and the punishment I would receive when I got home. Never once did the loss of acceptance, which served as my original motivation for buying/stealing the glove, come up as a point of regret. No, the only thing made of leather I was concerned about was my father's belt, which I knew would be placed strategically across my rear end before the day was through. In any event, what occurred on that summer day back in 1975 was a crucible experience for me. Never since then have I taken anything that I did not earn by the sweat of my brow. No other event short of my mother's death had such a profound effect on me.

The thing I want you to take away from this anecdote is that the crucible experience exposed what I actually valued most, not what I said I valued most. Had you pulled me aside on the way into the store that day and asked me if stealing was wrong, I would have most certainly agreed. As I said earlier in this chapter, what we discover after being confronted with such temptations is often disappointing, and it may surprise others and ourselves. In my case, how could a responsible kid with a paper route and Christian parents do such a thing? The fact is that my stellar upbringing was drowned out in that moment of moral inertia. Everything virtuous concerning the perils of stealing was smothered by a phalanx of possibilities: acceptance, approval, and the joy of possessing what I wanted without having to pay for it.

My story is a classic level one Red Zone situation, an example of how, given the proper conditions, otherwise good people can be tempted to do things contrary to their upbringing and perceived character. It takes a strong man or woman of God to face down such temptations. Thus, we should be slow to judge such people who do fall, because it is very likely that, put in the same circumstances, we would make the same poor choices they did. After all, apart from their high profile, I do not think the architects of the fictitious revenue enhancements used by Enron and a host of other companies are any different from you or me. They knew what they were doing was wrong from an ethical point of view. Still, they hung the golden rule on the scaffold of greed and proceeded anyway. They found themselves in a Red Zone, and they failed to convert. How many times have we done the same thing, only on a smaller scale? Such is the nature of fallen beings.

Types of Crucible Experiences

Virtually all crucible experiences can be categorized into three main types: mentoring relationships, insertion into foreign territory, and disruption and loss. We will examine each in turn.

Mentoring Relationships

The right mentor at the right time can change your life. Think of Luke Skywalker's relationship with Yoda in *Star Wars* or Frodo's relationship with Gandalf in *The Lord of the Rings*. In each story, the relationship between hero and mentor was an ongoing crucible experience that revealed the heroes' core values and challenged them to dig deep and become the kind of people they were destined to be.

One of the most powerful mentors in my life was a successful business-man and former athlete named Bill Noble. He was my mentor and coach from age thirteen to eighteen. My ability to manage the changes of forced racial integration in the 1970s was made far easier through his direction and support. Bill helped my friends and me in ways that none of us had knowledge of at the time. It was not so much that we talked about the realities of race and disadvantage; we simply focused on what we could become regardless of race. That may have been all that was needed.

Although my family lived in north Tulsa, my school—Thomas Edison Junior High—was located on the south side. So I had to get up as early as 4:30 a.m. to catch the bus. If I wanted to participate in after-school sports activities—which were my passion—it meant catching the "activity bus" home. Our football practices lasted much longer than the activity bus would wait, so it became necessary to find an alternative means of transportation. Unbeknownst to my teammates or me, Bill pulled some strings with the city of Tulsa and got them to change the route of one of their buses so that it would take us back home at the appointed time. This bus became known as the "8th and Greenwood" bus. It would be years before we knew who was responsible for that decision. Who knows where this motley crew—Jerome Calloway, Keith Morton, Alvin Liggins, Mark Anderson, Tyrone Center, and me—would have wound up had it not been for people like Bill who helped us do the things we were most passionate about doing.

You may wonder why our parents did not provide the transportation themselves. Some tried. But the socioeconomic realities of African-American life at the time were so numerous and pressure-packed that few parents had the means or the occupational flexibility to offer support. For example, my family owned a car, but my dad often worked late, so there was no way he could provide consistent transportation. The powder blue Galaxy 500 owned by Mark Anderson's father was on its deathbed. The only question was how costly the funeral would be. Then there was the Calloway's "grey bomber," a Chevrolet station wagon. It was not in much better shape. And that was pretty much how things were in my neighborhood.

In addition to helping out with our transportation problems, Bill took a particular interest in me. Later, he told me it was a conscious choice that he and his son, Scott, had made. Scott chose me as the kid he would like to "help out," as Bill put it. Clearly, they saw me as disadvantaged but possessing some unrealized potential.

My parents were my ultimate role models. They provided the foundation upon which every future opportunity and relationship would be built. But if I hoped to move beyond the limitations imposed by class and race, I would need some exposure to a new world of opportunity. Bill Noble was the conduit through which I gained it. Through Bill, I experienced so much of the "good life" that it created something to reach for, something tangible.

We would go waterskiing, camping, and target shooting. Later on in high school, I worked in his steel company and received excellent wages. Even before then, he helped my friends and me get steady work at the local Coca-Cola bottling company in the summer. This helped to bolster my sense of responsibility. It also gave me an appreciation for earning money as well as an understanding of what I didn't want to do for the rest of my life. I did have a paper route when I was much younger, but this was different. I was really on my own, fending for myself—as much as any fifteen-year-old can. It was liberating. And I had Bill to thank for it.

I do not suspect I would even be writing this book if I did not have Bill's influence in my life. It allowed me to observe a businessman in action. Again, the foundations of responsibility were established by my parents. My association with Bill merely gave me the opportunity to live them out in professional environments. This experience was not always easy, but it was priceless. And the timing of this mentoring relationship—which I am certain was engineered by God—was perfect and far-reaching. It was a crucible that utterly transformed the way I regarded my prospects as a young African-American male.

Insertion into Foreign Territory

Most of us will find ourselves operating in foreign territory at some point in our lives: a new job, a new relationship, or possibly launching a new business or ministry venture. Individuals who are able to extract insights from those experiences (particularly when such experiences are forced upon them) are the ones that show the most leadership potential. Such experiences are nearly always Red Zones. Whether or not they become crucible experiences is up to you.

Noted social psychologist Erving Goffman first introduced the concept of "total institutions" in 1961. Although Goffman gives some latitude when defining what a total institution is, they tend to be places like prisons, boot camps, and the like—any place where the individual's environment is totally controlled by an autocratic authority. In such places, you either adapt or you die. Goffman studied such extreme examples of environmental change so that people's coping mechanisms would be clearly apparent. Then he could extrapolate this behavior and apply it to more "normal" situations.

Football training camp could be regarded as a type of total institution. It is all about assembling a group of men with common interests, talents, and fears; putting them in a high-pressure, "make-it-or-break-it" situation; and seeing what happens. In the context of training camp, you will be exposed to new techniques, different ways of approaching particular defenses, and new systems and conditions. The limits of your tolerance will be tested as coaches flesh out their strategies against other coaches with big egos. Caught in the middle are the players—instruments, in many instances, of these orchestrated confrontations, all competing against each other for a limited number of spots. The social mechanisms players must employ to survive are complex. However, they must be mastered if you hope to walk the fine line of standing out from the crowd while still getting along with your peers. In addition to the pressure of "fitting in," players must live with the constant possibility of finding a pink slip under their door in the morning. Imagine living with that every night. Most forays into foreign territory are not as intense as NFL training camp, but they can have the same positive effect on your life if you let them.

Disruption and Loss

Death is the ultimate disruption. In the Introduction to this book, I discussed the passing of my mother and the series of introspective events that this loss triggered in my life. Finding meaning in a loss of this magnitude is a most powerful crucible.

Near-death experiences can also have this effect. My former high school coach, Tommy Thompson, whom I love dearly and remain close to today, suffered a major heart attack and had to undergo quadruple bypass surgery on April 4, 1984. Coach T, as I called him, was a Vietnam veteran. A two-inch-wide, forty-inch-long gash, caused by a mortar round, runs from his lower chest to the base of his stomach. It served as a visible reminder of how close he came to death. To make things worse, he was shot while being loaded onto the helicopter that was supposed to carry him away to safety.

After Vietnam, Coach Thompson became a teacher and a coach. He had a fireball of a personality, an ignitable sort. After the heart attack, however, it was clear to everyone who knew him that Tommy had changed completely. He became the antithesis of every one of the aforementioned personality traits. Tommy demonstrated patience beyond measure; nothing but love oozed from his spirit. To this day, we call each other randomly and tell each other how much we love each other. When I am in Tulsa, we greet with a big embrace and a kiss—real "man" stuff, I know. It's a beautiful thing.

After Tommy's heart attack, local sports legend J. V. Haney motivated Tommy to get up and do something about his situation. While it might seem an insensitive way to handle someone in Tommy's condition, it worked. Tommy thought he would never be active again, but J. V. Haney motivated Coach T throughout his recovery. Less than two months after his heart attack, he completed a fifteen-kilometer race and has remained an avid runner ever since. Tommy also began to think about doing things he had never done before. For instance, he and his wife, Connie, had never been to a Texas-Oklahoma football game. They took a gamble and went to Dallas without tickets. After standing in the rain, they managed to purchase a pair at an inflated price. But the price did not really matter to Tommy. Somehow, coming toe-to-toe with death at this point in his life released another level of appreciation for doing things that are worth remembering; things that constitute the spice of life: relationships, shared experiences, and struggles. Such is the potential of crucibles.

Crucible Experiences Are Painful but Necessary

Hebrews 12:11 says, "No discipline seems pleasant at the time, but painful. Later on, however, it produces a harvest of righteousness and peace for those who have been trained by it" (NIV). What is true of discipline is also true of crucible experiences. Crucibles are really a form of discipline, meaning they produce moral or mental improvement. They may not be a lot of fun at the time, but the long-term benefits are indisputable. The truth is, a price must be paid for anything worth having. Remember Thomas Paine's entreaty? "What we obtain too cheap, we esteem too lightly."[5] Said another way: "We value things according to the amount of effort we put into attaining them." It is difficult to walk away from something to which you have dedicated a great deal of time, money, or effort. Nations fall, visions are aborted, and marriages fail because people are too quick to throw in the towel at the first hint of trouble. Good leaders, those with the potential to become great, learn to embrace these difficulties to some degree, realizing, as the apostle James points out, that trials are the things that refine and strengthen our character (James 1:2–4). The development of perseverance and character is the first step toward scoring in the Red Zone.

Testing is necessary. Just as food and water make us stronger physically, tests have the potential to make us stronger both morally and ethically. How does this work? As you experience trials and temptations, you must exercise the correct responses to open the doors to improvement and success. Otherwise, the door to victory will remain closed. Like a bodybuilder, your moral muscles get stronger each time you exercise them.

The correct response to temptation is to do what God's Word says we should do in that situation: do not panic. This is an open-book test. Everything you need to know is at your short- and long-term memories' disposal. Of course, a prerequisite of its availability is your willingness to store that information there to begin with. That's right, if you want to benefit from the Word of God, you actually have to read it.

You may not enjoy crucible experiences, but denying them is tantamount to denying reality. It's far better to embrace reality and, with God's help, get through the experience rather than seek a way around it.

Crucible Experiences Are Unavoidable

Leadership experts Warren G. Bennis, Robert J. Thomas, and many others agree that there is a strong connection between great leaders and their ability to manage adversity. But how can we provide the leadership required during a Red Zone experience if we have never experienced the pressures and risks that accompany hard times?

Success is about more than minimizing pain. In fact, often the only way to achieve success is to embrace pain. Think of football players: they purposely put their bodies through intense pain during the conditioning process, because that is the only way to get fit. Even so, many people still try to avoid pain and trials at all cost. Indeed, much of what passes for successful life strategies today are built on avoidance ideology. They imply you will be able to achieve success by avoiding the requisite trials and temptations such a journey entails. What makes these offers so appealing is they offer a "zap" instead of a process. Instant success sure sounds a lot more appealing than the long, slow version. But most "shortcuts" are really dead ends or detours. The sooner you realize this, the sooner you can get moving down the road to true success.

How Do Crucibles Differ from Red Zone Experiences?

As I stated earlier, every Red Zone experience has the potential to become a crucible experience. Like crucible experiences, Red Zones expose our core values, they are necessary for success, and they are unavoidable. Whether or not a Red Zone experience becomes a crucible experience depends on how you respond to it. Implicit in the word *crucible* is a successful outcome. Red Zones are simply events. To qualify as a crucible, the event must alter the way you see and interpret a situation, the world, and your role in it. Subsequently, your behavior is changed in accordance with this new, altered view of reality.

Here are some basic questions to help you determine whether or not an event is a true crucible experience:

- Do you embrace the experience rather than avoid it?
- Do you learn something from the experience that produces fundamental changes in the way you view life and your place in it?
- Do you put that lesson into practice so that you do not just have a cognitive revolution but a behavioral one as well?

For example, the death of a parent is an automatic Red Zone that nearly everyone will go through at one time or another. When a parent dies, everything is shaken up. This leads to a profound emotional experience as you reflect on the brevity of life, regrets or joys you may have about your relationship with the deceased, and possibly the meaning of life and your place in it. However, unless this reflection translates into a fundamental shift in the way you approach life, it is not really a crucible experience. It is merely a Red Zone—an experience where the need for you to achieve your objectives has suddenly increased at the same time as the obstacles between you and your objectives have grown more formidable, your options for overcoming those obstacles have decreased, and time is running out. Some refining may have occurred, but not the transformational change that defines what a crucible is all about. The clincher is whether you emerge from the experience as precious metal or as the same, misshapen lump of iron ore you were to begin with.

Making the Most of Crucible Experiences

The following pointers are based on an article by Ellen Ostrow, PhD, called "When the Going Gets Tough, the Tough Learn Resilience."[6] With her permission I have distilled her list down to what I feel are the essential attitudes and behaviors one should develop and practice to make the most of any crucible experience.

Face Reality

People who make the most of crucible experiences understand and face the reality of their situation, even if it is emotionally difficult to do so.

For example, our friend Nehemiah could have downplayed the destruction occurring in Jerusalem. But after surveying the damage for himself, alone and under the cover of darkness, he faced the grim reality that Jerusalem lay in ruins. "You see the trouble we are in: Jerusalem lies in ruins, and its gates have been burned with fire. Come, let us rebuild the wall of Jerusalem, and we will no longer be in disgrace" (Nehemiah 2:17 NIV). Unlike many leaders today, Nehemiah saw no value in building artificial hype to inspire his followers to achieve their goal. As we discover later, Nehemiah was appealing to a chosen people's core values—love of God and love for their nation. More often than not, that is sufficient to ignite and sustain a worthy cause.

Make a Commitment

People who are committed to what they do are far more likely to benefit from crucible experiences than those who are not. If your work feels trivial or meaningless, it will be very difficult for you to persist in the face of hardship. But if you hope to experience success, to score in the Red Zone, you need to overcome this phobia. In this regard, I find these words from W. H. Murray particularly inspiring: "Until one is committed, there is hesitancy, the chance to draw back, always ineffectiveness . . . [then quoting Goethe] 'Whatever you can do or dream you can, begin it. Boldness has genius, power and magic in it. Begin it now.'"[7]

Resilient people often create their own crucibles as a way of bettering themselves or taking advantage of an opportunity. They are the sculptors of their life and career situations, not the sculptures. That is, they shape their situation; they do not allow their situation to shape them. Take initiative by identifying opportunities and then acting on them. Go beyond adapting to adversity and actively work to change your circumstances for the better. Try to identify and pursue opportunities for self-improvement, such as establishing relationships with mentors and acquiring needed skills. Develop a career plan. Seek a work environment that matches your needs, values, and skill set. Build a network of supportive colleagues, friends, mentors, and a professional coach to help you anticipate change and prepare for it.

In my senior year at Oklahoma, I played in two premier bowl games that professional scouts attended to evaluate future NFL talent: the Senior Bowl and the Hula Bowl. Seeing as I was a running back playing for a university that featured the running game, I knew the question scouts would be asking was, "Can this kid also catch the football?" NFL teams cannot afford to take on players with a limited skill set, because it is too easy to defend a particular player if he can only do one thing. During preparations for each game, I asked my head coaches if they would throw the ball to me and put me in kickoff return situations. The way I figured it, the only way NFL scouts would get their questions answered was for them to see me in catching situations. Both coaches agreed, and the results, thank God, were good. I caught a diving catch for about forty yards in the Senior Bowl, and I had a big kickoff return in the Hula Bowl. Mission accomplished.

When I became a free agent two years into my NFL career, the 49ers offered me a contract. If memory serves me correctly, the tape I sent them did not include one passing play. But coaches are like elephants: they have long memories. Sherman Lewis and several other scouts remembered my Senior Bowl performance and even recalled specific plays as we engaged in small talk during my visit. An organization like the 49ers, whose name is synonymous with passing, does not offer you a multi-year contract if you can't catch. Remember the mousetrap theory: if you can do the job, customers will already know something about you, usually before you know anything about them. So, be proactive, because you have everything to lose.

Develop a Sense of Humor

As a lawyer, Dr. Ostrow is acutely aware of the culture of the legal profession. It is extremely serious, but the fact is, you still need a sense of humor if you hope to navigate through such change and adversity. While it is vital for you to face the reality of your situation, it is also useful to see the absurdity in it. Humor is exactly what provides you with that perspective. Try to remember the crises with which you successfully coped and how enormous they seemed at the time. Laughing at how seriously you can take yourself sometimes helps us to create the psychological space needed to see alternatives you have not already considered.

Stay Focused

We will discuss this principle in great detail in Chapter 9, so consider this a brief primer. Have a clear sense of what you are trying to achieve, and use your goals and priorities to stay on track during turbulent times. Do not waste your energy on unimportant details or the "tyranny of the urgent." There are always temptations to lure you away from the task at hand. If you do become sidetracked temporarily, use your goals and core values to help you maintain your priorities.

Being a broadcaster at the network level carries with it a certain degree of celebrity. It's the illusionary aspect of what I do. I find it embarrassing that someone would hold me in any higher esteem or want my autograph simply because I am on TV. What I do find compelling about my work is the whole idea of a big studio: cameras, people, and resources coming together to put on such a dynamic event. The average individual has no idea how much effort it takes to do what we do. So when guests come in, predictably they linger and want to see what it's all about. It takes a fully engaged producer-talent relationship, however, to keep these experiences from becoming distractions to the extent that it compromises our ability to focus and do good television. A producer's challenge, among many, is the management of our preparation, which takes time. Failure to articulate thought in a concise and consistent way drives producers crazy. Achieving a sense for what we intend to say and how long it will take to say it—once live and on-the-air—is achieved in rehearsals. Anything that encroaches upon our rehearsal time—unscheduled visits—is a distraction and threatens the successful execution of a time-sensitive show. Missing a commercial break can cost more than any of us could afford to pay. Thus, talent must be aware of the *nature* of the producer's role and work together to meet his needs by engaging guests quickly and politely, then redirecting our attention to the preparation at hand. I've learned to adjust to all of this and still maintain a high level of focus. For me, studio work is a constant, real-time assessment of what is currently going on and what could possibly go wrong. From the time I get on the plane on Friday until I leave on Sunday—provided we do not have an NFL assignment—I am extremely focused as I process reams of college football information. That is the way I like it, and I suspect every professional does this to varying degrees.

Be Resourceful

Crucibles often require you to use whatever resources you can find. This includes your internal resources as well as those you can access from others, such as emotional support. Improvise. Be creative. Be willing to try something and see if it works. You can always discard it if it is not effective.

Be Flexible

Crucibles also demand that you consider a wide variety of options when addressing challenges. Rather than getting stuck repeating ineffective strategies, pay attention to obstacles and use them as information that a new approach is required.

Vision or mission statements can be powerful agents of purpose in this regard (more on this in Chapter 5). However, they must be flexible enough that everyone can own the vision. Imagine, for example, how much easier it was for the Levites to get on board with Nehemiah's vision for rebuilding Jerusalem once they considered the potential implications for their tribe. Remember, the Levites owned no land traditionally. Their income came from offerings of money they received for taking turns at the temple. The Levites also alternated in preparing for the daily sacrifices, singing, and providing musical accompaniment. If Jerusalem were destroyed, the Levites would go hungry. Suddenly, the idea of helping Nehemiah build the wall was not just his little project; it was crucial to their survival. Flexibility can keep an initiative, family, or company from tearing apart, particularly in the Red Zone, when unexpected forces rise up to prevent you from achieving your objective.

Structure Ambiguity

The uncertainty caused by crucible experiences can be minimized by organizing the information you have. Categorize and prioritize information in a way that allows you to approach challenging situations with a plan. Keep yourself from becoming overwhelmed by developing an organizational structure that enables you to evaluate approaches systematically according to their effectiveness. When you are systematic, you hold on to the important details and discard those that are irrelevant. You can also avoid retracing your steps and continue to move forward.

Football coaches are masters at structuring ambiguity. Nearly every aspect of their preparation is planned—each play, each route, right down to our pregame meals. The schedules leading up to the game are also detailed and specific. What players—particularly the younger ones—often perceive as restrictive actually makes their execution on the field more predictable.

When I was with the 49ers, each Saturday night before a game, our offensive coordinator, Mike Holmgrem, would hand out a sheet with the first fifteen plays he intended to call on Sunday. Rarely would he deviate from those "first fifteen." There were many advantages to scripting the first fifteen plays, not the least of which was how it enabled Mike to get a clear read on what the other team was doing. From his vantage point in the press box, he had a perspective that allowed him to see if the defense was responding the way he anticipated. If not, then he could make adjustments to the play list to exploit any weaknesses he observed in them or to compensate for any weaknesses he observed in us. Structuring ambiguity in advance makes real-time adjustments possible and creates the confidence needed to navigate Red Zone scenarios successfully.

Be Self-Aware

Transforming a Red Zone experience into a crucible experience requires that you stay open to the reality of the situation but also to the reality of your responses to it. The only way you can develop a self-improvement plan is through an honest assessment of your strengths and limitations and the kinds of assistance you need. Men often feel that they have to be able to do everything themselves. But don't be fooled. That is just the "path of least resilience."

Be Persistent

Persistence is crucial to navigating your way through crucible experiences. Being persistent does not mean never feeling discouraged. It means maintaining your focus on the goal in spite of discouragement or setbacks. Like a marathon runner, you keep going because you believe in what you are doing.

Develop Your "Emotional Intelligence"

Author Daniel Goleman, who pioneered this catchphrase, defines emotional intelligence as a set of skills, including control of one's impulses, self-motivation, empathy, and social competence in interpersonal relationships. Emotionally intelligent people see to the heart of the problem and are perceptive of interpersonal cues. They are assertive, willing to tell others about themselves, but they do so in a socially skillful way. When someone's emotional intelligence is well developed, people experience them as warm, caring, and compassionate. People like emotionally intelligent people and want to help them achieve their goals.

Obviously, it takes a certain degree of emotional intelligence to benefit from and survive any crucible experience. Qualifications, education, and experience are important. But I cannot think of anything I have ever achieved, either personally or professionally, that did not have some degree of emotion as its driving force. Predictably, the degree of my emotional investment in a certain activity corresponded to the degree of significance those achievements rank in hindsight.

Believe in Yourself

The belief that you can influence the circumstances of your life is essential to making the most of crucible experiences. This does not mean you think you can control everything. It means cultivating your ability to focus on what you can influence and control and not getting hung up on things outside of your control. It's the old "Serenity Prayer" made famous by Alcoholics Anonymous: "God grant me the serenity to accept the things I cannot change, courage to change the things I can, and the wisdom to know the difference."

Develop a Strong Sense of Purpose

Good leaders know what they are doing. However, great leaders know why they are doing it. This is the difference between merely living a vibrant, exciting life and living a truly purposeful one. People who succeed in the face of great adversity have a strong sense that life is meaningful, that there is a point to their existence.

This kind of vision is a hallmark of great leaders as well as survivors. The image of something meaningful provides you with an anchor to hold on to during turbulent times. It can transform an overwhelming situation into one that is manageable. I have no doubt that this is exactly what helped Nehemiah and his crew thrive during the reconstruction of Jerusalem and the reinstruction of his people. He understood Jerusalem's role in light of history. If Jerusalem was to be the city from which Jesus would emerge, it could not remain in ruins. Nehemiah worked as if Jerusalem's very existence and the fate of the Messiah rested in his hands. Such is the effect that crucibles can have on us. When faced with adversity, people who might be considered average otherwise can achieve greatness when they cooperate with a group that shares their core values—which are the subject of our next chapter.

4

CORE VALUES

Pillars of Strength, Predictors
of Success and Failure

It was a sportscaster's dream scenario: the bottom of the ninth, bags full with runners, and the winning run at the plate. With only seven minutes to go until we hit the air with the latest details of this Texas Rangers/Boston Red Sox game, I turned to my producer for an update. Just then, I saw one of our four camera operators, a young man, dash out from behind his camera, spin one of the floor monitors around, and pull out a video game controller from the drawer below.

"You've got to be kidding," I said to myself. I had been warned not to take this job opportunity by my CBS colleague Tim Brando. This was one of the rare times when I should have heeded his instruction.

I let the kid have it. In truth, I was more upset with those running the show, but he was the most convenient target for my anger. How could they permit a culture that embraced such unprofessional habits to develop?

Midway into the broadcast, an associate producer brought me some updated highlight information from another game in progress. The notes did not make any sense, so I asked her to put me in touch with the individual who had watched the game.

"*I* watched the game," she responded. "What's wrong with what I wrote?"

My embers were still smouldering from my exchange with the camera guy. "For starters, I'd kind of like to know who was on base. And while you're at it, can you tell me who was at bat? I could guess, but Yankee fans might not appreciate it."

Having just observed my exchange with the young cameraman, she no doubt thought that I was a jerk. What she actually called me, though, was much more offensive, but the same point was made.

The sad thing is, if you had asked me just prior to that event what my core value was in regard to treatment of others, I would have said something along the lines of the golden rule. But on that day, my version of the golden rule went something like, "Treat others as you wish to be treated as long as they effectively facilitate your success by making you look good in the eyes of others." How hypocritical is that?

This story is a great example of how the core values you verbalize often differ from the values by which you actually live. Sadly, it often takes a crucible experience like this one to reveal your core values for what they are. By then, you have usually done or said something to hurt others. But things do not have to be this way. Even in a Red Zone situation, the correct response can become instinctive and reflexive. But first, you must know what your core values are and why you hold them. That is exactly what this chapter will help you figure out.

A Soldier's Example

Established core values are what made former NFL player Pat Tillman the hero he was in the eyes of all who knew him. Pat was destined for greatness on any front. Already an established star on the gridiron, Pat walked away from a multimillion-dollar NFL contract to fulfill a lifelong ambition—to become an Army Ranger. He could have chosen the money, a life of luxury, and fame. But he was operating according to a higher core value: serving his country. Unfortunately, while on patrol in Afghanistan in April 2004, Tillman was killed in a fierce firefight. He was only twenty-seven years old. It goes to show that abiding by your core values may be the right thing to do, but it is not always easy, and it could cost you your life.

On ESPN's SportsCenter, Pat's father commented on his son's decision to walk away from football stardom to join Operation Enduring Freedom.

He said, "You only get a few opportunities in life to show your stuff . . . You either step up or you don't. If you don't when you should, that tends to eat away at a young man. And I don't believe that stuff goes away as you get older."

In a sense, I have a difficult time determining which is the greater tragedy: a hero dying while obeying his core values or that his obedience was so unique it warranted such special attention from the media. Don't get me wrong, in this instance the media did what they do best: they showed us, with words and pictures, what greatness really looks like and what each of us is capable of when we find ourselves presented with the same kind of decision Pat Tillman faced. The sad thing is that there are so few examples of people who choose the value over the dollar.

Once you can answer the "why" to any question, you are in rare air, able to soar above and beyond the mediocre. If not, you will just keep going through the same revolving door of disappointment, frustration, and failure, because you will never be convinced that your core values are the best of all available options. Every time you face a situation in business, family, or relationships—all potential Red Zone areas—without your core values in place, you declare your preference for defeat.

What Are Core Values?

Imagine you are leading a resource and development team at a large biotechnology company that is on the verge of a major breakthrough. After a year of work, everything hinges on your final contribution to the project. However, three weeks before your deadline, you are "head-hunted" by a rival corporation that offers to double your salary. There's just one hitch: you have only twenty-four hours to decide, meaning your part of the project will remain unfinished. If you leave, everything your team has been working for may be lost. If you stay, you miss out on what could be your next big break. What do you do?

Your teenage son wins the lead in the school play. He rehearses for weeks and has reserved front row seats for you and your family on opening night. That morning, your boss asks you to make an emergency flight to "put out a fire" in one of the firm's satellite offices. If you agree, not only will you miss opening night; you will miss the play's entire run. But if you refuse, you risk missing out on that promotion your boss has been dangling before you like a carrot on a stick. What do you do?

You've been trying for months to land a crucial account for your company, putting in tons of overtime and missing out on important family events as a result. Just when you think you've reached the breaking point, the prospective client agrees to your terms and signs the contracts. Elated, you burst into your supervisor's office expecting to be commended, only to discover he is in the midst of a phone call with the CEO, during which he takes credit for everything you've done. What do you do?

Each one of the scenarios above places two values in competition with one another—individual vs. organization, family vs. work, and recognition vs. success—and then asks you to choose one over the other. How you choose reveals a lot about what you consider to be most important in that situation and in life as a whole. Your choice reflects your core values. As I noted in Chapter 1 when I described the different levels of Red Zone situations you will face, your decisions in these circumstances also determine the type of person you will become.

Essentially, a core value is a belief about what is most important in life. Core values are to humans what roots are to trees: without them, we would fall down. Examples of core values include family, pleasure, financial success, power, integrity, and popularity. We all operate according to a set of core values, whether we realize it or not. Core values differ from person to person, as does the hierarchy in which we place them, but we all have them. The difference comes from the moral foundation upon which our core values are based.

Where Do Core Values Come From?

People draw their core values from a variety of sources. Let's examine a few of them here.

Self

Let's face it, we are all self-centered by nature. If something is in our best interest, we will do it. If not, we will need a compelling reason why we should. Even then, that compelling reason usually has our self-interest at the fore, as in "Pay your taxes or go to jail."

Family

Family is the primary socializing institution in society. In a family situation, core values are taught as well as caught. However, even though families serve as incubators for core values, they are not really a primary source, because our families, like us, all derived their core values from somewhere else.

Culture

Although families should be the primary socializing agent for children, many parents have abdicated this role to television, movies, video games, and the Internet. The truth is, a lot of parents have allowed themselves to be socialized by these cultural influences as well, so they do not even recognize what is going on with their children or stop to consider that it may be a negative thing. This creates a frightening situation where the blind is truly leading the blind. I am not one to advocate unplugging the computer or turning off the TV altogether. That would really be a clear-cut case of biting off the hand that feeds! However, I do advocate better monitoring of your children's use of these technologies and more personal discernment about what you take in yourself.

Education

In most high school and college classrooms, we find ourselves in an environment where Christian values are rarely advocated and are often refuted or ignored. This is not always the case, but it is no secret that the sphere of education has fallen under the control of humanists whose agenda is to eradicate any religious influence, Christian or otherwise, from our children's classrooms or textbooks.

Race or Ethnic Background

This is particularly important if you are a member of a minority whose struggle for identity and acceptance has defined your existence. If so, some of your primary core values may include acceptance, success, and disproving anyone who says you cannot or should not do what you are setting out to do. Each one of these core values can serve as a motivator to achieve or a barrier to success, depending on how you approach them.

Government

Government leaders, the laws and policies they create, and the lives they lead, always promote some kind of moral agenda. But it is not always one that matches up with Christianity. At their best, though, governments and politicians act as a strong moral force in society. And they should, seeing as many governments and legal systems—including our own—were founded on Christian principles.

Religion

Many religions offer a moral code of sorts for their adherents to follow. In the case of Christianity, our core values are based directly on God's character. Throughout history, God has given us some moral codes, such as the Ten Commandments and the entire legal code of the Old Testament. But when Jesus came, He explained that all of these laws, even detailed regulations about how to prepare food before eating it, were all based on two core values: love of God and love of neighbor. That's because the foundation of God's character is love (1 John 4:8, 16). By orienting your life around these two values, suddenly you realize an enormous code of laws is no longer necessary to regulate your behavior. When faced with a decision, all you have to ask is, "Will doing this thing demonstrate love for God and others?" If not, then the choice is clear.

"There Is a Way That Seems Right to a Man . . ."

Six years ago at age thirty-seven, WorldCom CFO Scott Sullivan was making $20 million per year. But at his core, Sullivan—born of middle-class blood in Bethlehem, New York—was an "average Joe." Even with millions socked away, he and his wife led an inauspicious existence. Then in 1998, the Sullivans started plans for a $15 million mansion in Boca Raton, Florida. It had to happen sooner or later. After all, who could blame him for wanting to reap some harvest from the good seed he had sown so faithfully?

Coincidently, just as Sullivan decided to reward his diligence, the bottom started to fall out of WorldCom. In an effort to survive the nosedive the telecommunications industry was suffering, this God-fearing, church-attending husband and father decided to list billions of dollars of day-to-day operating costs as capital expenses, giving the appearance that WorldCom was far healthier than it was. In other words, he "cooked the books." The truth? WorldCom was neck deep in debt to the tune of about $40 billion.

An Old Testament proverb states, "There is a way that seems right to a man, but in the end it leads to death" (Proverbs 14:12 NIV). Dependence on human wisdom is exactly what led to Sullivan's role in one of the biggest corporate accounting scandals in U.S. business history. In *The Cheating Culture*, author David Callahan speculates that Sullivan may have reasoned that he was doing a favor for the seventeen thousand employees and stockholders at WorldCom, even though that meant violating federal law. The question remains though: How could such a duplicitous perspective exist within the heart of a faithful churchgoer, learned Sunday school teacher, and confessing Christian?

The answer is simple: Sullivan lacked established core values. Sullivan may have invoked God in his interviews and in many of his corporate presentations, but his actions were clearly undertaken without God's council and influence. Once again, we see that you can talk about your core values all you want. But in the end, it's what you do—not what you say—that reveals the truth about what you consider most important.

Once You Reject God, You're on Your Own

The minute you cut yourself off from the only valid source of core values—God—you are back to relying on your own wisdom. You have moved from light into darkness, from absolutism to relativism.

Moral relativism is the belief that absolute morals—indeed, absolute truth—do not exist. Or at the very least, if absolute truth does exist, it's impossible to know what it is, because no individual or group can get an objective view on what exactly that truth is. We are all mired in our own limited perspective. This being the case, moral relativists—whose roster, I would argue, includes as many undeclared members as there are of the card-carrying variety—insist that everyone is in an equally valid position to determine what is and is not true. In fact, seeing as we all look at things differently, what may be true or good for one person may not be true for another. Or, what may be true or good in one situation may change in the next. It all depends on the circumstances, the individuals involved, and the objectives at stake. Thus, the overriding value becomes one of utility or pragmatism. Does it work? Does it feel good? Does it help you get what you want? Then go for it.

Many categorize this brand of thinking as "enlightened," because it prevents adherents from "lowering themselves" to the petty squabbles that divide people who hold dogmatically to a given set of beliefs or values. While I cannot deny that religious fundamentalism has done as much or more damage as relativism, ironically, you will not meet anyone more dogmatic than a moral relativist. As much as they hate to admit it, moral relativists do hold true to one universal truth or value, and that is "tolerance." The only thing not tolerated by these moral relativists is intolerance. Think that one through.

Doing Things God's Way Isn't Just Right—It Works

In twenty years of business and professional pursuits, I've found this truth to be operative. When I started doing things God's way, every aspect of my life moved exponentially in a positive direction. That said, there are still reminders—some of them visible—of the mistakes made and the sins committed over the years. Deciding to follow God's plan for your life does not absolve you from reaping what you've sown. I still kick myself over some of the business deals I've done with people of questionable character. I am not talking about obvious villains here but people who were undecided about their core values. But now, just give me five minutes and a couple of key questions, and that's all I need to determine if I should be in business with someone. It all seems so clear now. Perhaps you can relate. Once I learned with whom I should be in business and for what motives, my batting average improved substantially. Of course, deals still have to make sense from a business standpoint, but that's simply not enough. The deals I've taken the most thorough baths on have been the ones that looked the best.

This does not just apply in business situations. Think about your family. How would your family be transformed if you started parenting according to the two primary core values outlined by Christ: love of God and love of neighbor? You will not find any closer neighbors than your family! The same goes for your social life, your life at church, and virtually any other sphere of existence. Basing your life on God's core values will only lead to success, strong relationships, a good reputation, and every other good thing. The degree to which you are able to do good consistently is directly related to the fixed nature of your core values.

How Can You Determine Your Core Values?

In the business of broadcasting, getting a story first is all that matters. Someone in your organization must always be on watch, because you never know when the next big story will break. If you get it first, you can promote that fact to your viewers to remind them that you are *the* source when it comes to the dissemination of important information. For the viewer, this translates into trust and reliability. For the broadcaster, it translates directly to the bottom line: stations with highly viewed programs can charge more to their advertisers. As you can imagine, the battle for viewers is often fierce—and ugly. If ever there was a situation that seemed designed to expose your core values, this is it.

In 1995, I worked for KPRC-TV, a television station in Houston. One day, I received a call from a producer requesting that I "front" a story—provide the voice and physical presence to complete the elements of the story. No problem. I was told a cameraman and producer had acquired video of the construction efforts going on inside the home of basketball superstar Charles Barkley. Unfortunately, I quickly learned that the way they gained access to the construction was clearly unethical. Perhaps there would be a problem after all.

When the producer phoned me about this "good get," I asked if they had any sound from Charles. She said no. I suggested I call him up to get an interview. She balked at that notion immediately and confessed the video was acquired by less-than-honest means. Suddenly, I smelled trouble. If this story broke without Charles's knowledge, who would be the first person he and the Rockets would blame? It was a no-brainer. I was his neighbor. I worked for a television station. I realized I was in trouble whether I did this story or not.

Apparently one or both individuals suggested to the project manager inside Barkley's home that it would be okay for them to come in, invoking my name as a credible source and noting my friendship with Barkley. Indeed, I knew Charles. In fact, our backyards buttressed one another, allowing us to exchange pleasantries over the fence occasionally. Barkley had just signed with the Houston Rockets, and the organization was trying to keep his business as private as possible. But people are resourceful, and you can only keep these sorts of things a secret for so long.

I told my executive producer I did not feel comfortable fronting the story without Charles's knowledge and involvement. But she would not go for it. In the end, they decided to go with their "get" and use another talent to tell the story.

When the item hit the air, who do you think got in trouble with the Rockets organization? That's right, yours truly. I was convicted before I could defend myself. I did my best to explain what I knew about the matter, but to no avail. I went to my executive producer, who then informed the news director. I was told, "It will blow over. Don't worry about it."

At that point, I lost respect for our organization. Never once did it cross their minds that damage had been done to my reputation as a result. Players like Barkley are the ones I call on daily to get information and gain access to stories. Cross one and you've crossed most. I phoned the Rockets immediately and apologized on behalf of the station and me. Then I sent Charles's wife a dozen roses followed up by a personal visit. They accepted my apology, and we remain cordial acquaintances.

In my opinion, whenever a broadcaster's aim to ignite controversy supersedes its obligation to inform, it points to more than a momentary suspension of sound moral judgment. This is where the uneasy tension between the quest for ratings and core values often collides. In the end, management sets the tone, and its minions do what anyone without established core values would: cave in to the pressure to please.

The temptation to compromise my core values during this situation was immense. This was a definite level three Red Zone situation. By refusing to participate in this story, I was going against virtually everyone else in the organization, placing my reputation and possibly my job at risk. But I am also thankful for this experience, because it helped to confirm what my core values really were. In hindsight, I probably could have handled the initial exchange with management differently. I was just so hurt that they would so easily discount the incident's effect on my reputation and my ability to do my job. In the end, it really does not matter. I am a much better broadcaster, businessman, and person as a result of having gone through that ordeal. And I survived with my integrity intact, which means everything to me.

Examine Yourself

Apart from crucible experiences or Red Zones, another way to determine your core values is to do a thorough examination of your heart. Ask yourself some hypothetical questions like the scenarios I presented earlier in this chapter and answer them honestly. What is most important to you? On what values have you based your life? Take a look at the direction your life is going. What are your goals? What activities occupy most of your time? What are the areas of your life you tend to neglect? Who or what do you look to as your primary moral foundation? What do you spend most of your time thinking about?

Ask Others

If you have trouble being honest with yourself, try bringing other people into the equation, such as your spouse, your pastor, or a trusted friend. Judging from their observations of you, ask them to comment on what they think your core values are. If you are really brave, you might even try asking your children the same question. You will not get a more honest answer. But brace yourself. This kind of truth really can hurt.

Ask God

You might also try asking God for help. As the prophet Jeremiah says, "The heart is deceitful above all things and beyond cure. Who can understand what if you are paying 30 percent of your income on a home that may be in the "right" neighborhood but is totally inappropriate for your family's lifestyle? For instance, in an effort to gain status, you buy a condo in a downtown high-rise rather than a house in the suburbs, even though you have two young children who will now have to stay cooped up inside all day. If so, you are in violation of principle two. The same goes if you always opt for the cheapest item rather than the best item. You may save money in the short term but, as the saying goes, "Buying cheap gets expensive." So, as you can see, spending is not as simple as you might think.

Giving. If you hang out in church circles at all, no doubt you will have heard about the concept of "tithing." Originating from Old Testament times, this is the practice of giving the first 10 percent of your income to God (via the church) as a way of showing thankfulness to Him and, secondarily, to support the church's ministries.

While this was the practice in Old Testament times (and, some would argue, during the early church era), in no way are we obligated to abide by this principle. After all, we are no longer under the Law but under grace. That means we are free to give as little or as much as we want. Now that you are free from the burden of guilt, let me also say that I think 10 percent is an excellent starting point for giving. Did you catch that term— "starting point"? I do not wish to reintroduce the guilt factor, but I do want to remind you of a key financial principle found in Scripture: "Remember this: Whoever sows sparingly will also reap sparingly, and whoever sows generously will also reap generously" (2 Corinthians 9:6 NIV). Do you think you can out-give God? I don't. Do not let fear of financial ruin prevent you from giving generously. In fact, generosity is your best hedge against such calamity. Trust me: I speak from experience.

Another point on giving is to make sure you are investing your giving funds wisely. I support the Juvenile Diabetes Research Foundation (JDRF), which applies nearly eighty-five cents out of every dollar to finding a cure for Type 1 diabetes. Any organization can say they are "searching for a cure," but they may not be doing it in the most efficient manner. JDRF's record is unassailable in this regard. Not surprisingly, this organization was started by parents whose children are afflicted with the disease. What I am saying is, do your research. A generous heart is one thing. But generosity tempered by wisdom can turn base metals into gold.

Vocationally

A number of different attributes will help you establish traction on the job. I have chosen to unpack just a few of the most important ones here.

Diligence. Cyclist Lance Armstrong has reached the status of icon—allowing him to transcend his sport and enter the consciousness of the general public—because of his diligence and determination. His story, beating testicular cancer to win the Tour de France a record six times, is simply incredible. Four of those titles came after his diagnosis and subsequent surgery to remove one of his testicles. Brain surgery followed that procedure. The cancer had spread throughout his body. One of the doctors that viewed the cloudy haze on his X-rays shook her head in disappointment, convinced Lance would not make it another six months. Less than four years later, Lance's doctors declared him cancer-free. What happened in between that allowed him to come back and win was diligence and determination (not to mention the best medical treatment money could buy).

The grunt work that leads to victory is often missed by the masses as they celebrate an athlete's public success. But to the athlete, the moment of victory is but a brief pause in an otherwise grueling journey. Beginning in late summer, Lance cycles at least thirty-five hours a week. In February, Lance transplants his routine to Europe, increasing his hours and pace on the bike. By spring, he is climbing the Alps in the thinnest of air with an eye toward the Tour in July. Meanwhile, most of his competition has been resting. In a classic interview with ESPN, Armstrong said, "Every year I say, look, the preparation for the next tour starts when this one is over."[9] Some might consider that obsessive, and perhaps it is. But if your aim is high, your preparation must match. The good news is, neither Lance nor any other remarkable athlete has the market cornered on diligence and determination. You can find that proper balance that yields superior results in your individual and corporate pursuits as well. It is just a matter of deciding how serious you are about achieving your objectives.

Professionalism. When I think of professionalism, I think of dependability, showing up no matter what. My dad is one of the most professional men I know. Recently, I asked him where his work ethic came from. He told me that in nearly fifty years of work, he missed only two days. With stunning detail, he recalled the circumstances that led to those two missed days. One was a car accident. The other was weather related. My dad's sister Louise is the same way. As I write, she is seventy-two and as fit as a fifty-year-old. She can also count the number of times she has missed work on one hand.

Of course, professionalism means more than attendance, but if you look at the track records of people who are successful, showing up is always part of the equation. I missed two games during my NFL career. On one of those occasions, Brad Brown—one of the best trainers in the NFL—recommended that I be deactivated because of an injury. I cannot recall specifically what the injury was. But I will tell you that I cried publicly for the first time because of that. I do not have some heroic explanation for why I responded in that way. The fact of the matter was, I was only operating at about 50 percent. Brad knew this, and, as the trainer, was obligated to tell the coach that I would probably be more of a liability to my team than an asset that day. Still, I struggled with the thought of not being in my place. I do not know exactly where that feeling comes from, but I think my father's example has something to do with it. Gaining traction in the area of professionalism starts with an example of what professionalism looks like. Shoot for a higher standard if you desire, but never aim lower.

Networking. Of all the positions I have occupied in the world of television broadcasting—which is a lot—every single one has come about as a result of knowing someone in the business. I have made some of these connections in formal networking environments and others in more informal settings, such as parties. I am not much for the party crowd, but I do see the value of being where the players are. There is also no shortage of organizations to which I can and do belong, such as AFTRA (American Federation of Television and Radio Artists), NABJ (National Association of Black Journalists), and NFLPA (National Football League Players Association), among others. In total, I am a member of seven organizations and am an active participant on three boards as a director. That is my limit. I know mine, and you should know yours. Networking can easily burn you out. There is virtually no limit to the organizations to which you can belong. But effective networking is strategic. Throw your nets where the fish are.

Clearly, Jesus Himself was a proponent of having relationships with people of influence. Luke 2:52 says, Jesus "grew in wisdom and stature, and in favor with God and men" (NIV). The vertical component of traction was important to Jesus, but to fulfill His mission on earth, Jesus had to develop traction on a horizontal level as well. When we refer to Jesus, we use a number of names, but I have not heard Him referred to as a master "networker." Remember though, He was the one who charged twelve fishermen to go "fish" for men. Sometimes when someone tells you that he caught a bunch of fish, you probably struggle to take his word for it unless he has pictures. In Jesus' case, there are over two billion Christians on the earth today, and it all started as a result of one man who networked with twelve people. There was no online technology to assist Him. It was solely a word-of-mouth deal. Imagine that: Jesus was hip to networking over two thousand years ago.

Spiritually

Establishing traction on a spiritual level involves four main activities: prayer, fellowship, meditation, and reading God's Word.

Prayer. A most valuable truth my mother taught me was that God is always "speaking," always pursuing us. Let me explain: I consider the words in the Bible to be inspired by God. Therefore, I refer to what I read there as "hearing from God." When I read the Bible, words often jump out at me, resonating within. At those times, I am hearing from God. Call it a "lightbulb" moment or whatever you prefer, but when it happens, something special occurs deep inside.

Unfortunately, we are not always willing to listen when God speaks. Often, the time when we are most apt to listen is when we are undergoing the most difficulty, carrying the heaviest load—entering a Red Zone. We tend to go our own way until we encounter obstacles we do not think we can handle on our own. Thankfully, helping us establish traction in a slippery situation is

God's specialty. How does this happen? Through the most natural of human reactions in the face of adversity: prayer.

Prayer is not guesswork. Prayer is not wishing or looking to your lucky stars for a favorable outcome. Prayer is a high-probability exercise, a powerful tool no leader should do without. It is free, legal, and it works. What other motivation do you need to pursue it?

There is just one catch: prayer becoming a high-probability exercise is conditional. On what? Relationship. Try walking into one of Credit Suisse/First Boston's worldwide offices and asking for a $20 million loan on the spot—no references, no prior history of working with the bank or any of its officers. Sounds absurd, does it not? Then why would you approach God through prayer in a similar fashion?

I do not know about you, but I cannot just walk up to an individual with whom I have not actively cultivated a relationship and ask for a favor of any significance. Borrow a pen or hold the door, no problem. But borrow $20 million? Forget about it.

I have banking relationships in which I can share a vision, fill out some paperwork, and we are off to the races. But that did not happen overnight. It took a lot of time for me to establish a track record with that particular institution and the individuals in charge. In a similar way, you should not wait until you find yourself in a Red Zone situation to begin developing your prayer life. I am not saying that God does not respond to last-ditch prayers. But He is not like some sort of cosmic vending machine or panic button that you hit whenever you get in trouble. God is a person, complete with feelings, intellect, and a will. You are wise to keep that in mind when you pray.

Prayer provides more than just the initial traction needed to get up to full speed on a project. Prayer is something great leaders like Nehemiah do throughout their leadership assignments, because they understand the precarious nature of the situations they face. In Nehemiah's case, he genuinely believed that someone capable not only of hearing but assisting him as well was on the other end of his cries to heaven. So, rather than become like a flag, blown whichever way the unpredictable winds of change decided to blow, he undertook prayer as a preemptive measure and used it to shape his leadership challenge instead.

Predictably, Nehemiah prayed in the following situations:

- when he first heard of Jerusalem's condition (Nehemiah 1:4–11)
- when he faced King Artaxerxes to make his request to be allowed to go to Jerusalem and make repairs (Nehemiah 2:4)
- when he faced direct opposition (Nehemiah 4:4, 9)
- when he faced false accusations (Nehemiah 6:9)
- when the work was completed (Nehemiah 13:14)

Nehemiah knew that prayer and work went hand in hand. Sometimes it was a quick one-line job, and other times, such as when he first got word of the state of Jerusalem, it was a lengthy lament. In fact, Nehemiah's opening prayer in Chapter 1 is the longest individual prayer recorded in Scripture, if you exclude the Psalms.

What happens when we pray? You might be relieved to know you do not need to have a storehouse of good deeds in order to pray. In fact, quite the opposite is true. Prayer, as I am learning, will actually produce good actions on our part. As a result of honest, thoughtful prayer, your attitude changes for the better, giving way to a higher probability of producing better actions.

Think about it. Have you ever known a person whom you considered harsh or hard to get along with to acknowledge that he or she prayed habitually? Bitter people do not pray, or, said another way, people are bitter because they do not pray. You can live a more peaceful and productive existence if you make prayer a fundamental part of the leadership equation instead of a last-ditch alternative when you get into trouble. This is what Paul was saying in his letter to Timothy: "I exhort first of all that supplications, prayers, intercessions, and giving of thanks be made for all men, for kings and all who are in authority, that we may lead a quiet and peaceable life" (1 Timothy 2:1–2). The essential nugget Paul drops right off the bat is that prayer comes before everything else, as it did with Nehemiah. With your busy schedule, awesome leadership responsibilities, and so forth, you cannot afford not to pray—for no other reason than the peace it produces.

Perhaps you are thinking, *I have managed to do pretty good so far without praying.* May I suggest that you could do more than just "manage"? I do not believe anyone who is serious about achieving success, by any definition, sets out with mediocrity as his or her goal. I am suggesting here that, through prayer, there is more available to you if you want it.

If you do not pray first, it becomes impossible to gain full access to a wellspring of wisdom and knowledge that can be infinitely valuable in your leadership role. As God says in 2 Chronicles 7:14, "If My people who are called by My name will humble themselves, and pray and seek My face, and turn from their wicked ways, then I will hear from heaven, and will forgive their sin and heal their land" (NIV). Your "land" is your home, your family, your place of business—everything over which you preside and have interest. God has so arranged His relationship with us that you can sit down, stand on your head, drive in your car, or simply sit and talk with Him anytime you want.

Where do you start? How about the beginning of your day? The first thing I do in the morning is say, "Good morning, God. This is a day that You have made. I am excited about that fact. God, will You be my personal CEO and lead me through this day? What do You want me to do? With whom do You want me to do it? How do You want me to do it? Lord, lead me, guide me, and help me to be obedient to that guidance." You don't have to pray in the morning. Some people find it easier to pray at night or at various other points throughout the day. I prefer the morning, because it gets me focused on God as soon as I get out of bed, if not sooner.

After I pray that prayer, I become comfortable with the fact that I have asked God to do this and that He has answered that prayer in advance, even before I prayed it. As I go through the day, I strive to do things as He expects me to do them, and I keep my eyes and ears open—in faith—for how He will answer my prayer. Other times when I pray, I just listen. In fact, it is good to get in a habit of just listening to God and meditating on what He has already told you through His Word.

It is impossible to understand truth and reach God if you do not pray. Of all the "tractive" exercises I have shared in this chapter, prayer is the most important, bar none. Can you still be successful by secular definitions without it? Perhaps. But, as Jesus said, "What good is it for a man to gain the whole world, yet forfeit his soul?" (Mark 8:36 NIV).

Fellowship. For an increasing number of people, attending church is shifting from "mandatory" to "optional." This is part of the "problem of privilege": the more we prosper, the less we feel we need God and each other. What we fail to note in such instances is that we owe all of our success to God, because He is the One who keeps our hearts beating and our lungs full of air. Attending church and worshipping God is one way of giving thanks for this. If anything, our privileged position in life should make us more thankful than ever. But somehow it does not seem to work that way. We say we do not have time for church. Why? Perhaps because the best tee times are on Sunday morning. Or maybe Sunday morning is your only time to sleep in. I am sorry, but those simply do not qualify as excuses. As I have said before, we always find time for the things we value most. If you go golfing instead of attending church on Sunday, what you are really saying is that you consider golf more important than God. And if that is the case, you have to ask yourself which God (or god) you are really worshipping—the Creator of the universe or yourself? And as far as the sleep factor goes, I can understand where you are coming from, especially if you have young children who keep you up half the night. But enough churches offer late morning or even Saturday evening services these days that lack of sleep is not really an excuse either.

If you want to establish traction spiritually, you cannot afford to go it alone. You need to spend time with like-minded individuals in church, in small group settings, and one-on-one with your pastor and other spiritual mentors. Through this interaction, you can give and receive encouragement, direction, education, and friendship. If you still think you can follow God all by yourself, remember: even the Lone Ranger had Tonto.

Meditation. By this term, I am not advocating that you take up yoga or find yourself a mountaintop and park there for a while. But I do think it is important to quiet your mind periodically and spend time reflecting on God's Word, life in general, and your place in it. Often, God chooses such times to speak to us, because our minds are finally quiet enough for us to hear Him. If you are not comfortable with the concept of meditation, start by choosing a Scripture verse or passage and mulling it over in your mind. Even if you have read the passage several times before, ask God to give you new insight into it and what it means for you. You will be surprised at the results.

Bible Reading. Reading and studying the Bible is another highly "tractive" exercise. The individual who is convinced of Scripture's relevance beyond that of good literature has discovered an endless power supply. Through reading the Bible, you gain not only fuel for your life's mission; you also become a beacon of light for others—such as your children—who are searching for someplace to rest and refuel before setting out once again on this great journey called "life." You should study the Bible to gain traction in your own life; but the greater value in gaining this sort of traction is that it enables you to pull others along as well. Their weight actually gives you a reason to pull. A locomotive is of little value unless something is hitched to it. Remember: if you do not read, you do not lead.

If you do not read the Bible regularly, I urge you to begin doing so now. Start small, perhaps a chapter or a few verses per day, and then build from there. Choose a book of the Bible that interests you or, better yet, ask God where you should start. You will be amazed at how quickly His Word becomes your Word.

Every Step of the Way

Anyone who has lived through winter in the Northeast knows that putting sand or rock salt on only the first step of a flight of stairs covered in snow or ice will not cut it. If left untreated, each step poses a danger. Therefore, to make the entire incline negotiable, each step must be treated. Similarly, you cannot get away with establishing traction at only the initial juncture of a leadership challenge. It must be established and reestablished each step of the way, from the earliest stages of preparation to the last phase of execution. Traction may be required on one level or many. You may need additional funds, brighter talent, or stronger strategic relationships. Whatever the need, apply the principles of traction I have described in this chapter, and you will get it.

8

CREATING CONNECTIVITY

Stellar Leaders Connect with the Human Condition First

The game could not have been going better. It was 1992, a play-off match between my team—the Houston Oilers—and the Buffalo Bills. We were leading the Bills 28–3, thanks to four touchdown passes by Warren Moon, and we were not showing any signs of slowing down. I suspect the cold, wet weather on that January day aptly reflected how the Bills felt as they trudged back to the dressing room at halftime. It was the Oilers' sixth consecutive play-off appearance. Everyone thought this was the year we would finally make it to the game of games, the Super Bowl.

A Record We Never Intended to Set

When we came back after the half, we broadened the spread early in the third quarter to 35–3. But then things started to unravel. Over the next seven minutes, the Bills—without the help of stars Jim Kelly and Thurman Thomas, I might add—scored four unanswered touchdowns. With only three minutes left in the game, the Bills' backup quarterback, Frank Reich, tossed one more touchdown pass, making it 38–35 for the Bills. We were stunned. Minutes earlier, we had the game in the bag. Now we were fighting for our lives.

In a desperate effort, we managed to put away a field goal with only seconds to spare, forcing an overtime period. But the Bills responded with their own field goal in overtime and chalked up a 41–38 win. Just like that, our Super Bowl dreams were over.

Now it was our turn to hang our heads as we filed into the locker room. We had set a record as the team to have the largest lead before giving up a loss in NFL history. That included all games, both regular season and play-offs. No one had ever lost as badly or as thoroughly as we had after having as big a lead. And let me tell you, it hurt.

A Multitude of Symptoms, a Single Result

So what happened? How could we go from the top to the bottom in seven minutes flat? I can answer that question with one word: connectivity. Or, rather, three words: lack of connectivity.

To begin with, the stadium was loud. Normally, if there were any adjustments to be made to our defensive formation before the ball was snapped, Jerry Gray, one of our defensive backs, would communicate these changes verbally to the other players. But on the first fateful Bills scoring drive of the second half, the crowd was so noisy in Rich Stadium that all Jerry could use to communicate were hand signals. Unfortunately, one of our safeties, Bubba McDowell, misinterpreted those signals. Thinking Jerry wanted to switch responsibilities, Bubba ran forward when the ball was snapped rather than dropping back, as he would normally do. Instead of taking Bubba's place, however, Jerry ran forward as well. With the field left wide open behind them, Bills wide receiver Don Beebe ran the ball thirty-seven yards to score a touchdown. After the first touchdown, the defense did adjust, but they still did not do things right. Suddenly, the Bills scored again. Reeling from the abrupt reversal of fortune, we continued to make changes, but every time we did, the Bills still got through.

Another problem that contributed to this inability to concentrate was arrogance. As Bubba says, "My grandmother could have covered this team, at least the first half version we saw." Few people master the art of focusing when all the indicators suggest you do not have to. As Nick Saban, head coach of the Miami Dolphins, says, "The greatest threat to future achievement is your last greatest accomplishment." Indeed, the victory party—or previctory party, in this case—can often be the biggest Red Zone of all.

Counting the Cost

Breakdowns in connectivity can be annoying. But when you enter a Red Zone situation, they can be devastating. In the above example, not only did we suffer embarrassment and miss our chance at the Super Bowl that year; our defensive coordinator, Jim Eddy, was fired, along with several assistants. Eddy was replaced by the legendary Buddy Ryan, and everything became a circus after that.

We did improve defensively under Buddy. But he was a tyrannical, egocentric personality. He actually threw a punch at Kevin Gilbride, our offensive coordinator, on national television. Buddy was upset that Kevin kept passing the football when we had a slight lead in a tough defensive battle. Buddy felt we should protect the lead and run the football instead, using up the clock. I hate to admit it, but he was right. We were not passing very well. By refusing to run the ball, we were actually working against ourselves. But I still do not think a strong right hook to the chin was the best way to communicate that point—or any point, for that matter.

Connectivity Can't Wait

You cannot wait until you are in the midst of a Red Zone to establish connectivity. If you hope to thrive in the Red Zone, you have to start establishing connectivity with your people now. It must become automatic and reflexive during times of relative peace so that when you enter a Red Zone, you are not trying to figure out how to connect with your people in the midst of the fray. The forces inherent to the Red Zone will put you off your game before you even realize what is happening. Pace is not the only thing that picks up in a Red Zone though. Emotions flare, egos rage, and fear kicks in. Like an open wound, Red Zones are harbors for infection. Whatever was growing inside you and your team beforehand—the good, the bad, and the ugly—comes into full view when the pressure is on. That is why preparation is so important.

If you are prepared, you can simply revert to the systems and methods you have already established during "practice." This all sounds well and good. But what is this magic elixir called "connectivity"? How does it differ from mere communication? And how is it established?

Connectivity: A Definition

Obviously, connectivity involves communication. But it also includes something more: relationship. It is "communication plus." Connectivity means connecting with the human condition first. More than a mere exchange of information, connectivity establishes a reciprocal, personal bond between you and whomever you are trying to communicate with, thus providing a relational context for the information being exchanged. Without relationship, communication becomes nothing more than an exchange of facts. You may still get your message across, but instead of gaining the willing cooperation you desire, you will elicit nothing more than reluctant compliance. With relationship, communication is transformed into a dynamic, two-way exchange of thoughts and feelings that motivate your team to buy in to your vision and put everything they have into helping you realize it. And we all know you want that.

God: The Ultimate Model of Connectivity

To find the ultimate example of connectivity, you need look no further than God. The Trinity—Father, Son, and Holy Spirit—are intimately entwined, so much so that even though They are three persons, They are one. With God, it is all about relationship. Communication never occurs outside of this context. The best part is, He desires to have this same level of connectivity with us, as Christ expresses in John 17:11: "I will remain in the world no longer, but they are still in the world, and I am coming to you. Holy Father, protect them by the power of your name—the name you gave me—so that they may be one as we are one" (NIV).

Connectivity is made possible only by the implementation of a multifaceted infrastructure that takes into consideration the most common human concerns and addresses them accordingly, allowing for a free-flowing exchange of personal and relevant information. Practicing connectivity will improve attitudes, performance, and, ultimately, the bottom line.

Staying connected with your team is difficult in the best of times. But maintaining it while in a Red Zone is a constant battle. Nehemiah struggled with this throughout the rebuilding process. However, by constantly encouraging his people, settling disputes, gauging the pace of work to make sure people could keep up, keeping track of people's level of satisfaction with his leadership, and constantly reorienting them toward the goal, he met their needs and achieved his objective on time. His secret? Connectivity. He knew that as long as his people knew that love was his motivating factor, it did not matter if he was admonishing, educating, or confronting them. They knew he was doing it for their own good and for the greater good of the nation. They trusted him that much. Sound like the kind of results you are looking for? Then read on!

The Greater the Proximity, the Greater the Connectivity

When considering how to establish connectivity with your team, it is always wise to ask how your team members prefer to send and receive information. A good rule of thumb is, the greater the proximity, the greater the connectivity. Most people prefer a face-to-face meeting to a phone call or a fax, especially when dealing with serious issues. That's because all of the senses are engaged in the communication process, leaving less room for misunderstanding. As author John Kao says in *Jamming*, "You project substance loudest and clearest in person."[10]

Generally, the medical profession is adept at performing their core mission, which is helping people improve their health. Their success in this area is due in part to their definition of *communication*: "The process by which information and feelings are shared by people through an exchange of verbal and non-verbal messages."[11] There are two components of this definition to which I want to draw your attention: First, that communication is understood as an exchange of information *and* feelings, not just one or the other. If all you communicate are facts, you will elicit either blank stares or the bugbear of organizations everywhere—reluctant compliance. If all you communicate are feelings, you may feel better personally (or worse), but you will have no insights into how to deal with a particular situation. Get information and feelings working together though, and connectivity begins to happen. Before you speak, make sure you engage your heart.

Second, this definition also recognizes the importance of verbal and nonverbal messages. Once again, this is why physical proximity is so important to connectivity. Effective salespeople know that a face-to-face encounter with a potential customer or client is the most effective way to generate a sale. That's because they are not only communicating with words; they are also using body language, vocal inflections, and other cues to create interest in their product or service. Talking to someone on the phone still allows you to use your voice, but all of the nonverbal cues are gone. And if you simply write or send an e-mail, even less about you and your product is communicated. With each degree of separation, the opportunity for relationship and, thus, connectivity is impaired.

Even so, increasing proximity is not always the best solution. Some people may find being in close proximity to their supervisor intimidating. Tongue-tied and nervous, their ability to connect may be inhibited rather than enhanced. Rather than meet face-to-face, such people may prefer to communicate in writing instead. That way they have time to prepare and edit their thoughts before sharing them with others. In such cases, greater connectivity may occur when proximity is lessened—but only to a point. As Lou Holtz said, "Distance is to love [or any relationship] what oxygen is to fire. A little bit is okay, but too much will snuff it out." Your job as a leader is to get to know your team members well enough so you can begin to make these sorts of determinations and connect with your people accordingly.

For example, there is nothing my broadcast partner, Tim Brando, enjoys more after a stressful day in the studio than going out "for a pop," as he calls it, and rehashing the day's events. I'm not wired that way, but I realize how immensely valuable this is to him. Sometimes "Timmy B" just wants to flesh out what we could have done to make the show better that day. You've got to love a guy like that. Usually, we just sit in the hotel bar or go to our favorite restaurant. I may have a merlot or just water; but that's not really the point. The issue is, I am connecting with him in a way that is best for him. Our destinies are inextricably entwined as coanchors at this juncture of our careers. So it is in our best interest to do whatever is necessary to take our game to the next level. These little powwows are an excellent way for us to dialogue regarding the more important aspects of our existence beyond work. It may not be my ideal way of communicating, but I have only seen good things happen as a result.

Go Directly to the Source

In journalism, no tool establishes greater credibility than the direct quote. With it, the writer connects the reader, viewer, or listener directly to the source of an idea, a point of view, an action, or an event, thus maximizing the level of connectivity. Listen to a news anchor give a report about the devastation wreaked on 9/11, for example, and you may be moved. Watch and listen to a survivor tell his or her tale of survival, and you may be moved to tears. In the first case, information has been exchanged, but there are already several degrees of separation between you and the source. But in the second case, the information is the same; however, it is accompanied by feelings, images, and nonverbal cues. It has come directly from the source.[12] As emotional beings, we immediately feel a personal connection with that person or event. For that brief moment, we feel we have developed a relationship with that person, and we respond accordingly.

Connecting with the Human Condition in Times of Crisis

By Chapter 5 of Nehemiah, our model leader has a major crisis on his hands. Sanballat and Tobiah—kingpins of the region and Nehemiah's archenemies—receive word that the rebuilding effort is progressing nicely. A strong and prosperous Jerusalem, however, is not in their best interest. For them, it is the equivalent of a brand-new, sprawling mall being constructed right next to their family-owned enterprises. They will not get to share in those profits. In fact, they may be put out of business altogether, and they can't have that. So, along with the men of Ashdod, they plot war against Jerusalem.

Concerned citizens living outside the city walls become privy to the enemy's intentions and warn Nehemiah. In a preemptive measure, Nehemiah responds by posting guards at the most vulnerable areas of the wall. The men posted there work and defend around the clock. But the pell-mell pace and intense preparedness required by these dual objectives eventually takes its toll on the workers. What happens next is a both familiar and predictable response in any Red Zone.

The men and women repairing the gates and walls around Jerusalem begin complaining openly about their economic situation. They are working hard and sacrificing for the common good of Jerusalem. Yet some of the richer Jewish people are taking advantage of their poorer brethren, charging extremely high interest rates on loans during a famine. This is all happening in addition to the added threat of imminent invasion. The poorest of the workers have had to mortgage their fields, vineyards, and even their homes to get out of debt. Many have even been forced to sell their children into slavery so they can feed their families. They are powerless, because they own nothing. Their condition is critical. A level four Red Zone.

Nehemiah's response is similar to when he accepted the challenge to restore Jerusalem. First, he ponders the matter in his mind. Then he responds decisively. He calls an assembly to accuse the nobles and officials, saying, "What you are doing is not right" (Nehemiah 5:9 NIV). Now, that's clear communication. This is not flowery speech intended to placate a powerful populace. It is simple, straight talk that cannot be interpreted as anything other than what he intends: stop doing it!

Nehemiah continues: "Shouldn't you walk in the fear of our God to avoid the reproach of our Gentile enemies? I and my brothers and my men are also lending the people money and grain. But let the exacting of usury stop! Give back to them immediately their fields, vineyards, olive groves and houses, and also the usury you are charging them—the hundredth part of the money, grain, new wine and oil" (Nehemiah 5: 9–11 NIV).

Nehemiah knew it was unlawful for Jews to treat their own people in this manner (Exodus 22:25). He also knew that truth presented in love demands a response from a believer. Additionally, Nehemiah was aware that the threat of rebellion existed if the nobles did not obey him, so heeding his words would be, if you will pardon the expression, in everyone's best interest.

Look at what happens next when a man of faith moves with the right mix of righteous indignation and a mandate from God: "We will give it back," the wealthy Jews respond. "And we will not demand anything more from them. We will do as you say" (Nehemiah 5:12 NIV).

Now let's examine this situation: Nehemiah could have written the wealthy Jews a letter. He might even have sent an envoy to relay his message to them. But Nehemiah judged the situation to be so dire he needed to address them face-to-face. Connectivity was established, and the results speak for themselves.

Connectivity Must Be Established with Multiple Constituencies

Another point worth making here is that Nehemiah was successful in resolving this conflict because he was well connected to both constituencies—the wealthy and the common workmen. In the end, he sided with the workmen. But I can guarantee his rebuke would not have been accepted by the well-to-do unless he had previously demonstrated a concern for their interests as well. The action Nehemiah took was for the good of the entire community. Both groups recognized this. Later, Nehemiah connected with a third group of people, the priests, when he had the wealthy Jews solemnize their oath to no longer take advantage of their brethren. That way if they went back on their word, they would no longer be facing Nehemiah's wrath; they would have to deal with God directly. And none of them wanted to do that.

As a leader, you also have multiple constituencies with which you need to connect. If you are a businessperson, these constituencies include your employees, management, clients, suppliers, and possibly even board members and shareholders. Also do not forget your family, friends, and, of course, God. Like Nehemiah, you must work at keeping in close touch with all of these groups. That way when you enter a Red Zone, you will not have the additional problem of sorting out relational issues in the midst of another crisis. Keeping your ear to the ground like this will also alert you to problems, like rebellion, even before they manifest themselves, possibly allowing you to avert potential Red Zone experiences.

More Than a Moment

As I hinted above, connectivity is about more than the actual moment of communication itself. To function well in the moment, as Nehemiah did, you must get to know your team on a deeper level, even outside of the work situation. You must establish systems of communication that keep the channels open, such as regular performance reviews and even more casual meetings, such as lunch dates. Otherwise, even your efforts to establish connectivity may start working against you. But make sure your efforts to develop connectivity do not impinge on your employees' already burdensome schedule. For instance, a weekend staff retreat may cause more angst than anything because the single mother on your team has to line up babysitting for the entire weekend.

Additionally, the more ways you are connected to your team, the stronger the bond between you and them will be. This sort of bonding is crucial if your team is to function as a cohesive unit during a Red Zone situation. An "at work" relationship is one thing. But think about how connectivity with your team could be strengthened by relating to them on a social, recreational, or spiritual level as well. Of course, connecting on all of these levels with every team member is not always possible or ideal. But even a small effort made in some or all of these areas will only serve to strengthen your team and your position as leader.

Keys to Establishing Conductivity/Connectivity

Some metals are more conductive than others. On a scale of 0 to 100, silver ranks 100, with copper at 97 and gold at 76. Because of its high conductivity rating, silver is commonly used in electrical circuits and contacts. Silver also has other specific advantages as a conductor: it does not spark easily, it is relatively lightweight, and it is slow to corrode. What great qualities to possess if you are in leadership!

Like metals, leaders can also be classified as poor conductors, average conductors, or excellent conductors. It all has to do with how well information flows back and forth from you to your team. It should be obvious that Red Zone situations demand highly conductive leaders. We are talking about how well the leader can transfer key ideas and agendas with followers and visa versa, thus unleashing a free-flowing exchange of thoughts, ideas, and concerns.

Conductivity requires more than memos and meetings to discuss company objectives. Before you go there, make sure you've connected with the human condition first. What are your team's collective needs and concerns beyond the immediate setting? I'm not suggesting you can solve every extenuating personal dilemma that followers may have. But the bank manager would be wise to connect with an otherwise valued employee who routinely comes in twenty minutes late before taking disciplinary action. Find out what the problem is. You may find your interpretation of behavior is far from the truth.

Tommy Books, a friend of mine who is senior vice president of a bank in Houston, found himself in this precise dilemma. He was troubled with the habitual tardiness of an otherwise excellent worker, indeed a model for others. Rather than punish the individual, however, he decided to connect with her. As he spoke to the young woman, she explained it was not possible for her to get to work until 9:20 or later each morning, because the distance from her child's day-care facility and the bank simply would not allow it. So Tommy gave her the option of staying thirty minutes later each day—a simple solution she accepted willingly. The result was a sense of confidence on the part of the young woman that her boss was looking out for her. And there's no better way to establish employee loyalty than that!

As this example demonstrates, being a conductive leader is not about demonstrating your personal communication prowess or parading your authority. It's about connecting with the human condition first. It's about serving, not lording your authority over others. Remember, the greater the grind, the greater the need for effective communication. A Red Zone situation is not your time to shine. It's time to model the very behavior you want your team members to emulate.

Responding in the Opposite Spirit

One of the foundational teachings of Loren Cunningham, founder of Youth With A Mission (YWAM), one of the largest Protestant missions organizations in the world, is called "responding in the opposite spirit." What he means by this is when someone comes at you in a spirit of fear, for example, you should respond with exactly the opposite spirit, which is love: "There is no fear in love. But perfect love drives out fear" (1 John 4:18

NIV). The concept of responding in the opposite spirit is predicated on Christ's teaching on how we should respond to our enemies:

> You have heard that it was said, "Love your neighbor and hate your enemy." But I tell you: Love your enemies and pray for those who persecute you, that you may be sons of your Father in heaven. He causes his sun to rise on the evil and the good, and sends rain on the righteous and the unrighteous. (Matthew 5:43–45 NIV)

The apostle Paul echoes this teaching in Romans 12:19–21 when he urges us to overcome evil with good.

A number of things can disrupt your ability to connect—fear, pride, selfishness, a controlling spirit, criticism, comparison, busyness, impatience—but each one can be overcome by responding in the opposite spirit. It is all about character. Abstinence from wrongdoing or repression is not enough. You must replace your appetite for what is wrong with an acquired taste for what is good and just if you hope to achieve sustainable growth. You must respond in the opposite spirit. If someone comes to you in a spirit of fear, distrust, or insecurity, respond in love. If people know you care about them, they will feel safe enough to loosen their grip a little on the steering wheel and allow you to take control.

If you are confronted with a spirit of pride, respond with humility. Like a soldier on the front lines of battle, if you go in low, there's less chance of you getting hit by a stray bullet. There's a lesson here for all of us: respect the gifts and contributions of your team members or be prepared to engage in a perpetual and costly search for qualified replacements.

When dealing with selfishness, respond with generosity. It may take time, but by modeling this virtue, sooner or later the hot coals you're heaping on their heads will become so unbearable they will begin to adopt an attitude that puts the needs of others ahead of their own.

The need for control is really a manifestation of fear or insecurity, a messiah complex, a belief that you are the only one who can do things right. The response? Freedom. The best way to combat a controlling spirit in yourself and others is to consciously give away responsibility or tasks, even if that means they will not be done exactly as you would like. This may sound counterproductive on the surface. But I'm confident that as you release your people to do what you've hired them to do—without your micromanaging over their shoulder—their productivity will increase, your organization's capacity for innovation will be enhanced, and your overall working environment will improve.

Criticism is best countered with encouragement. This does not mean correction cannot still happen, but, as I've already stressed, it must be done constructively. Being diligent to point out what your people are doing right before you get into how things can be improved will ensure your comments are taken as suggestions, not condemnation. In my business experience and leadership capacities on the football field, I've observed that encouragement is not needed nearly as often when laboring with people of character and purpose. Of course, we all could use an "attaboy" from time to time, but people of purpose fully comprehend what the reward is and can identify its importance to their personal objectives. Provided what you are working toward represents a core value and you have a reasonable chance of realizing your objective-sufficient resources, it will take more than a brisk wind to blow them off course. Individuals who are able to internalize objectives, to align their thoughts and actions to achieve a specific end, are way ahead of the competition. There are occasions, however, when a word from the leader is just what they need to press on.

Finally, the antidote to impatience is, you guessed it, patience. Like love, patience is a characteristic of the fruit of the Spirit: "But the fruit of the Spirit is love, joy, peace, patience, kindness, goodness, faithfulness, gentleness and self-control. Against such things there is no law" (Galatians 5:22–23 NIV). The ability to wait until all the facts are in, to persevere, to listen before you talk, is vital to establishing connectivity. That does not mean sitting around and doing nothing. Rather, in the words of a former college professor, it means "always in haste, never in a hurry." Knee-jerk reactions are not the stuff of which connectivity is made. In most cases, it takes time before the whole picture becomes clear. Only then will you know what action should be taken and be able to take that action decisively.

Restoring Connectivity

By this point, you may be thinking, *All this talk about connectivity and its importance is fine. But what if connectivity has already broken down in your organization? What should you do then?* I can think of no better place to search for a solution than the Bible, specifically, in the words of Jesus Christ.

"There Was a Man Who Had Two Sons . . ."

Luke 15:11–32 records Jesus' famous "Parable of the Lost Son," a story meant to illustrate God's acceptance of those who turn away from Him. In this story, the younger of two sons demands to receive his inheritance early. Not wanting to indulge his son but realizing he will not be denied, the father agrees. No sooner does the young man get his inheritance than he is off to the city, taking part in all sorts of debauchery.

It does not take long, however, before he runs out of cash. Then, almost on cue, a famine hits. Destitute and alone, the young man is reduced to feeding pigs for a living—one of the worst jobs imaginable in the Jewish culture, because pigs were considered unclean. He is so hard up he even envies the food the pigs are eating. But no one offers him a bite.

On his knees in the muck, drooling over a pile of rotten pea pods, the young man finally comes to his senses. Even his father's servants do not live like this. Although he no longer feels worthy to be called a son, perhaps his father will at least welcome him back as a hired hand. Anything would be better than this. With this plan in mind, he cleans himself up and heads for home.

While he is still a long way off, his father spots him. What do you think he does? Order his servants to chase his son away? No, instead, he runs out to meet his son, throwing his arms around him and kissing him. I can just imagine them collapsing together in a heap on the ground.

When the dust clears, the young man backs away, his head bowed, unable to accept his father's forgiveness. He pleads with his father to allow him to work as a hired hand, but his father will not hear of it. Instead, he orders his servants to bring his son the best robe, to put a ring on his finger, and to put sandals on his feet. Then he makes arrangements for the biggest party their farm had ever seen.

Why such joy on the part of the father? Why wasn't he angry? As the father exclaims in response to the objections of his older son, "This brother of yours was dead and is alive again; he was lost and is found" (Luke 15:32 NIV).

A Four-Stage Process

If ever there was a picture of connectivity breaking down and then being restored again, this story is it. Even though the young man lived in his father's house and enjoyed all the benefits associated with such a position, it was not enough. He wanted more.

Sound like anyone you know?

Committing perhaps the worst affront a child can commit against his or her parents—thanklessness—he rejected his father's love and demanded his own way. His father could have resisted, could have warned what was about to happen, but he was wise enough to avoid a battle he could not win. Despite the protests of his older son, he knew the only thing that would teach his wayward son was experience.

Sure enough, after living through the consequences of his actions, the young man finally wised up. Thus began a four-stage process that eventually restored connectivity between him and his father.

Confession. If you read closely, you will notice the first step was confession. Alone in the muck with the pigs, the young man finally admitted he had made a bad choice. It's unfortunate that we often have to hit rock bottom like this—endure a crucible or Red Zone experience—before we can see things clearly. However, sometimes we simply need to come to the end of ourselves before an honest desire to do what is right can be achieved. We will remain in the muck until this happens.

Repentance. Once the young man had clearly outlined his mistakes, the next step was repentance. To repent means to turn away from sin and toward God. That's exactly what this young man decided to do. He would leave his life of indulgence behind and go back home, even though he was doubtful about the reception he would receive.

Forgiveness. When he did arrive home, however, he was in for a surprise. Before he could even voice his apology, his father was all over him, demonstrating the third step in the connectivity restoration process: forgiveness. Even though the son had sinned greatly against his father, his father chose to show him mercy rather than judgment, grace rather than condemnation.

Reconciliation. The fourth stage followed immediately. It's amazing what can happen when we are willing to swallow our pride, isn't it? All was forgiven. Father and son were united once again. Connectivity was restored.

A Lesson of Hope

While Jesus intended this story mainly to show God's willingness to forgive us for our mistakes, it also encourages us to believe the same sort of reconciliation can happen in any relationship. If, as a leader, connectivity has broken down between you and your followers, there is still hope. Connectivity can be restored.

The road to reconciliation may not be easy. There may be those who, like the older brother in this story, say you do not deserve to be forgiven. But if you walk this road—confession, repentance, forgiveness, and reconciliation—you can rest easy, because your conscience will be clear. Complete connectivity may not be restored in every case, and it might not happen right away. But that is not always in your hands. Do what you can do; then commit the situation and the other people involved to God. Eventually, situations—and people—have a way of coming around.

9

FINDING FOCUS
The Vector Approach

Few skills are as important as your ability to focus. Whether you are a leader in business, church, or at home, you must learn how to juggle a number of tasks and responsibilities simultaneously. Drop just one ball, and you can bet the others will soon be bouncing around your feet. As a leader, you cannot afford to lose focus in the midst of an important task. Too many people will be affected adversely as a result. In this chapter, I will explain how to stay focused on your game plan in the midst of all sorts of pressures and distractions. Once you learn the techniques and strategies I will share, you will be able to establish and maintain maximum focus so you can keep all of those balls in the air.

The Vectors of Focus

When medical scientists speak of "vectors," typically they are referring to insects as carriers of a disease entity. But I would like to use the term in its mathematical or aeronautical context as a way of describing the direction and momentum of a moving body. Specifically, I would like to turn the word *vector* into an acronym that describes six elements that collectively point toward a vector sum of "Focus." They are:

1. **V**alues,

2. **E**nergy,

3. **C**ourage,

4. **T**alent,

5. **O**rganization, and

6. **R**esources.

Together, these elements will produce the kind of focus necessary for maximum productivity and sustained success in any pursuit.

Values

Our values determine the object of our focus. By now, you should know that it is impossible to remain on the proper heading or vector in life without strong core values. Values are like the North Pole, keeping our compass fixed on our desired destiny. In Chapter 4, I talked about how you must know what your core values are before you can achieve purpose. Having a general sense of right and wrong is not enough, just as having a general sense of your destination will do you no good if you are trying to get somewhere by plane or by car. Like Scotty on *Star Trek*, you need the proper coordinates. Otherwise you risk beaming down on the wrong planet. And we all know that rarely led to anything good for Captain Kirk and company.

More importantly, you need to know why you hold on to your chosen set of core values. Until you can answer that question, you can never be certain the things on which you are focusing your time, energy, and resources are the right ones. Thus, you will be tempted constantly to abandon your focus and answer such fundamental questions for yourself.

Relativism: Society's answer to the focus equation. Making our struggle to focus all the more difficult is the fact that we live in a society that is suffering from a major lack of focus in the area of core values. Instead of basing our nation, our institutions, and our personal lives on a common moral foundation, we have opted instead to put the locus of decision in the individual. Thus, we find ourselves in a situation where the very notion of truth itself is being challenged. What is "true" for you may or may not be "true" for me. As I mentioned previously, the only absolute seems to be that there are no absolutes. All of this sounds a lot like the situation Israel found itself in during the period of the judges: "In those days Israel had no king; everyone did as he saw fit" (Judges 21:25 NIV).

The problem with this type of thinking is that it assumes humans can be trusted to be inherently good. But how much more evidence is needed before we come to grips with the truth that humankind is at enmity against good? That is not to say we are not capable of "good" acts or even sustained periods of unselfishness and exemplary gestures of kindness. But throughout history, humans have also demonstrated an unimpressive aptitude for evil. Lacking historical perspective, however, each subsequent generation loses a measure of understanding needed to remain alert to the slow but certain erosion of our moral underpinnings. We are like a pilot who may be only a degree or two off his desired heading when he sets out. But the farther he flies, the farther from his intended destination he travels. All of this points to the need for America to refocus on its individual and collective character and adjust its course before it can move forward with confidence.

Energy

Staying focused on a given task requires tremendous energy. At times, you will be tempted to give up or give in to distraction. But you can persevere if you follow some of the principles and tips below.

One of the keys to maintaining a high energy level is to do what you love. This should arise naturally once you begin to focus on your core values, which give rise to your passions. In Chapter 10, we refer to passion as the fuel of success, the intense emotion that compels action. If you are pursuing your passion, you will not have to work at maintaining focus. In fact, you will need to discipline yourself to stop focusing on a given project when other obligations demand it.

Passionate people, those who are in love with their vocation, are like enriched uranium. They can produce exponential amounts of energy. Did you know that just one pound of enriched uranium can power an aircraft carrier for years? One pound of enriched uranium is smaller than a baseball. Consider that it would take one million gallons of gasoline to fuel an aircraft carrier for the same period of time.[13] One million gallons of gas would fill a cube fifty feet square. That is as tall and wide as a five-story building.

The "hub and spoke" approach. Even if you are pursuing your passion, at some junctures it may be necessary to do something that is not your ideal job. Short of kings and princes, no one ascends to dream positions without interim stops along the way. How can you sustain focus in such situations? Simply by remembering that with a little creativity, virtually any task can be sculpted into a stepping-stone along the path to success.

In this regard, I prefer to take a "hub and spoke" approach to pursuing my passion. Marketers use this approach to build brands and sell products. For example, before her fall from grace, Martha Stewart was a definite "hub." That is, she formed the center of the wheel that was (and is) Martha Stewart Living Omnimedia. Her name or brand had become so well established through her publications and TV shows that you could plug pretty much any "spoke" into it, and the item would sell. Want to peddle bed sheets? Put Martha Stewart's name on them. How about kitchenware? Same thing. Gardening tools? You get the picture.

Once you discover your passion, you can take a similar approach to your career. For example, you could say that the hub of my career is football. This is my passion. The first spoke I plugged into this hub was "player." Simultaneously, however, I also plugged in a spoke labeled "broadcast journalist." Subsequently, I have added "sports analyst" and, now, "author." While this book is not about football specifically, the principles and concepts it contains were definitely formed in part by my experiences on the field.

Looked at another way, you could say that another one of my passions is *communication*. This could also be regarded as a career hub. Some of the spokes on this wheel are similar to the spokes sticking out of my football hub, such as "broadcast journalist," "sports analyst," and "author." However, you can also add: "radio personality," "journalist," "public speaker," and "voice-over talent." These latter four areas have also arisen out of my passion to communicate. The medium may change, but the message and the passion remain the same.

I encourage you to approach your own career in the same way. Ask yourself the following questions:

- What is your hub? What is your passion, the fuel that drives your ambition?

- Which spokes fit best? Once you have determined your passion, what are some ways you can go about pursuing it? For example, if your passion is writing, what sort of writing do you want to pursue: articles, screenplays, novels, poems, reviews, opinion pieces, interviews, comedy, ad copy, nonfiction books, radio, television, technical manuals, travel writing? All of these are potential spokes that can be plugged into the hub of your passion.

- Which spokes are primary? Which are secondary? With all of the options laid out before you, determine which options are primary opportunities and which are secondary. You can determine this by your level of interest in each area as well as your abilities and the opportunities available to pursue each one.

- Which spokes should be added first? Last? If your goal is to become a screenwriter but you do not have any connections in the film industry, which other form of writing could best facilitate that transition? Novel writing is one option, because many novels today are adapted into film. An entirely different option would be celebrity interviews, because this would allow you to make connections in the industry. Still another option is writing film reviews, because this will help you to understand what makes films work.

If you take this approach and do a good job of networking and developing your talents, you should feel reasonably good about the future prospects of landing that better gig sooner rather than later. In the meantime, keep one eye on the present and the other on your future. Create mental images of what will be, and use them to fuel you until you reach your preferred destination. I imagine what fueled Nehemiah as he sifted through the rubble and debris of Jerusalem was an image of what Jerusalem could and would be if they all worked together to achieve God's vision. With an unfailing God who had given them every indication that He would hold up His end of the bargain, Nehemiah knew they could not lose.

Beware of the Sandwich Game. If a football player's career has lasted any significant length of time, he has faced what we call "sandwich" games—games that fall between the present day and the future game on which you really want to focus. These games, in which your team is the decided favorite, can present a tremendous challenge to your ability to focus.

Situation: Your present opponent does not have a single player on their roster that your coach would trade for one of his. Looming two weeks away, however, is the game you have had circled on your calendar since the season ended a year ago. Perhaps it is a division foe—these twice-yearly meetings tend to be breeding grounds for the types of confrontation that fuel rivalries—or maybe something occurred in your last meeting to which every team member took offense. Whatever the case, the game you must play this week really does not matter, because you are playing an inferior opponent. So you look past it to the big game. Big mistake. While you're focusing on tomorrow, that so-called "inferior" team is taking you to the cleaners. A good coach will quickly identify activity consistent with "look-ahead" behavior and warn his team not to let their vigilance slip.

Take a break. Even people who are doing what they love have to take a break sometimes. You need to learn how to recognize when it is time to rest or change activities. When you push yourself past your energy threshold, you should not be surprised if and when things begin to grow fuzzy. Consider taking a break when you experience:

- a mental block
- a sense of reduced motivation
- particularly high levels of tension
- an inability to concentrate
- a personality clash with a coworker or superior

A well-managed break achieves three things:

Gives your faculties a rest: If you have been crunching numbers or engaging in a task that requires a single technical ability, change things up. It is like rotating the tires on your car. To extend each tire's life, you move them around. The good news is, changing gears does not mean productivity comes to a halt; it means you are simply engaged in something different.

While with the 49ers, my former teammate Matt Millen used to call our weekly training camp fishing excursions "Mandatory Fun." We had this shallow pool, about thirty yards by twenty yards, in which we would put catfish and various sundry items. Then we starved them for about four days. When we finally took the guys fishing, there was not much sport in it, because the fish were ravenous. It was either bite or starve. As contrived as this experience sounds, it was a positive distraction that helped maintain our sanity in the dog days of training camp.

Releases physical stress and tension: Sometimes I have sat at this desk or in my favorite chair at the bookstore for so long that my legs have gone numb. When I get up to stretch, I get a bonus by laughing at myself, because my forty-year-old body behaves more like a seventy-year-old's until I get loosened up. If you are stuck at a desk, stand up and stretch periodically. Do a few push-ups. Go for a walk during lunch hour. Get the blood pumping to your extremities again, especially that all-important extremity: your head.

Increases oxygen intake: Throughout a typical day, few of us use our lungs to our full capacity, and yet there is a direct correlation between oxygen intake and energy output. Take a few deep breaths every hour as a way of restoring your vitality. You will be surprised at how a couple of deep, into-the-diaphragm breaths will restore your alertness and enliven your entire body and mind.

Courage

My favorite scene in *The Wizard of Oz* is when the wizard yells, "Silence!" In response, the cowardly lion, so-called king of the beasts, promptly high-tails it all the way down the hall and out the window. It is a classic scene, but it also proves a point: without courage you simply cannot focus on what you have been put on this earth to do. You have heard it said, no doubt, that courage means acknowledging that fear exists but still possessing the ability to move forward. To be honest, people who do not get scared from time to time frighten me. It means they are either ignorant, not stretching themselves to their full potential, or they have settled on the status quo and vowed to protect it at all costs. Every forest you enter—relationships, work, education—requires the quality of spirit that enables you to face danger, pain, suffering, and setback without succumbing to fear. Notice I did not say that you need to be free from fear. Just avoid succumbing to it and move ahead anyway. That is the true nature of courage.

Talent

In the next chapter, I talk about how passion is the fuel of success. If passion is the fuel, then talent is the machinery that it enables to chug along, bringing us closer and closer to our goals. Talent's relationship to focus is twofold: First, developing your talents requires that you focus on them. Raw talent is one thing, but unless it is developed through a disciplined regimen of training and education, it will remain unrealized. No one gets drafted into the NFL or any other major sport on raw talent alone. Like Tim Robbins's character in *Bull Durham,* a pitcher who was long on ability but short on discipline, we must learn to tame and control that raw talent before we can move on to the big leagues.

Once you have developed your talents to a certain extent, a remarkable thing happens: you begin focusing on them less and less. Why? Because they have become so second nature that you no longer need to. You have reached the level of unconscious competence (more about that in the following chapter). This frees you to focus completely on the task at hand. Of course, you never truly "arrive" when it comes to your talents, and constant improvement is a must. But rather than spend all of your time in training, you are now ready to try your hand at a real game.

An increasing focus on talent. Historical and future indicators clearly suggest that for years to come, *talent*—defined as "possessing an unusual, innate ability to perform some task or activity"—will be prized higher than ever before.

In a piece written for Spencer Stuart, a Chicago-based concern specializing in senior-level executive search, merger, and acquisition services, Richard A. Smith and Jim M. Citrin point out that the rising interest in talent can be attributed to the following three causes:

1. The quality of professional jobs: They have grown steadily while the number of professional workers has not kept pace over the same period. This is a trend that is projected to accelerate over the next several decades.

2. Wall Street's progressive placement of higher importance on intangible assets, such as intellectual capital and strength of management. Hypercompetition, globalization, and progressively more dynamic markets have increasingly highlighted human capital as a corporation's most valuable asset.

3. Despite the economic volatility of the final quarter of 2004, unemployment of professional workers remained low.[14]

In summation, the trend over the last thirty years shows that more companies view talent as increasingly valuable. They are vying for a shrinking pool of executives, most of which are already working for someone else. The result: an increasing appreciation for the value of professional talent. So make sure you develop yours.

How's your talent quotient?

In addition, you do not have to demonstrate exceptional talent early on to be successful. After all, even Michael Jordan failed to make the varsity basketball team during his sophomore year of high school. If your long-term objective is to reach the highest level of your profession though, something distinguishable must emerge eventually, as it did for Michael. There is no question that Michael had the raw talent. His ticket to the big leagues was hours of practice as he refined his game and improved his weak points. When he returned to school the following year, not only did he make the varsity squad, but the following summer he was scouted by University of North Carolina coach Dean Smith. Michael's career was anything but smooth sailing after that, but we all know how it ended up.

The surest way to stay at or near the top is to "be like Mike": keep your gifts sharp and your nose clean. As one of my former coaches was fond of saying, "I know a lot of truck drivers that can run a 4.4 forty, son." I do not mean to disparage truck drivers; theirs is a noble profession. Our nation would literally grind to a halt without them. The point is, speed is just one characteristic of a good runner. You also need vision, instincts, strength, mental toughness, and stamina. Talents often operate in clusters like this, which means you cannot get away with developing just one.

Talent is not everything, and you do not need the lion's share of it to win. But you would be well advised to surround yourself with talented people who do possess a liberal measure of it. In Chapter 11, I talk about the importance of delegation. The ability to match tasks with talents is often the difference between failure and success. That is certainly the case in football. What separates the good defensive and offensive coordinators from the great ones is a knack for delegation: the ability to know whom to match up against whom. I might add that successful delegation does not mean the people you select are perfect. They are just better—or perhaps more available—than you are for a particular task. The difference between success and failure can be small. And talent, or lack thereof, can tip the scale one way or the other. Whether that talent comes from you or someone you appoint is irrelevant to the greater objective.

Organization

With so much information flying at us at once, knowing how to filter and process that information is just as important as knowing how to use the information itself. Organization is the art and science of creating a structure or system that allows you to classify and arrange information in such a manner that chaos's ability to return is severely impaired, allowing you to focus on the most important tasks at hand. A well-maintained organizational system will allow you to achieve maximum efficiency with the time you are allotted. Among other things, getting organized will:

- Free you up to focus on the really important projects: your passion and developing your talents, the hub and spokes of your career. When items central to your work are in place, you can locate what you desire with due haste. Leave the "hunting" to big game enthusiasts.

- Prevent your self-esteem from being compromised. Getting organized will also prevent your family, coworkers, clients, and friends from doubting your credibility and effectiveness.

- Breed peace of mind. When closets, drawers, shelves, and desk files are a mess, it can lead to frustration, because you are unable to locate important documents or that favorite garment. Eliminate these minor stressors from your mind before they derail the major projects on which you should be focusing.

Do your homework. Every organizational task requires a period of research and preparation. This is where you win or lose on both micro and macro levels. To draw a football analogy, training camp is the time when the methods, strategies, and general philosophies that will carry you through the regular season are put into place. This is when coaches try new plays and tactics they have been scheming during the off-season. One thing I can tell you though: if something did not work during training camp, chances are great that it will never be attempted during the regular season. There is too much at stake. Better to stick with what works. If you go down, you do so doing what you do best.

For the most part, the first portion of our halftime shows on CBS are formatted—not scripted, but structured—with little room for improvisation. The "vamp" or "fill" on the other end is just the inverse: a little bit of structure, a whole lot of flying by the seat of our pants. Our producer, Vin Divito, is in both Tim's and my ear giving us details regarding where we are going next. Can you imagine trying to count money and hold a conversation at the same time? Try doing that with a couple million people watching at home, and you will get a sense for what my job is like. Needless to say, focus in such situations is very important. There is no time to learn as you go. You simply have to do it. This is unconscious competence at its best.

The key to success in my line of work is to do your homework. It is all in the preparation. If I know my material cold, I should be able to talk my way out of any situation while being informative and entertaining. These days, you just cannot have one without the other. Our preparation must focus on the information that is most likely to make it to air, but we try to look at everything. We are thinking "big picture." If there is a win or a loss, what does it mean? We simply do not know which information will wind up on the floor and which will make it to air, so we have to make sure all of our bases are covered. In the same way, never content yourself with doing "just enough" on a particular job. Always go a step beyond what is expected or required. You never know when that extra bit of research or work you did will come in handy.

Become an "environmentalist." Most creative disciplines require some measure of space to conceive of ideas and solutions. Just as a couple must plan to come together to conceive a child, individuals seeking creative ideas must plan a time and a place for creative thinking to occur. Is there a place you can go to become "pregnant" with purpose? Is there a place that lends itself to creative thought and imaginative possibilities?

Start by looking around where you are presently. On a scale of one to ten, rate the atmosphere in terms of its conduciveness to your ability to focus. Presently, I am in a popular bookstore, and, to be quite honest, right now it is rather noisy. At any time, however, the environment can change. This can become a place where I can get quite lost in my studies. While a bookstore may not sound like the ideal working environment for you, as much as is possible, find a place or places where you can achieve maximum concentration and focus. I have heard of writers who have certain locales that trigger their writer's muse. For instance, I know the late Alex Haley wrote most of *Roots* while traveling in a boxcar. Although it clearly worked for him, thankfully I have not had to resort to anything like that—yet.

Find something you can dance to. Music is another way of creating a focus-rich environment. Whenever I strap on my headphones, I am transported instantly into whatever world my music creates for me. Sometimes I select different kinds of music according to the specific client or project on which I am working. When I work out, it is inspirational, hard-charging. When I am writing, it is usually softer, more reverent, something conducive to receiving subtle messages and ideas.

Sometimes, though, nothing can beat silence. Often when I am writing, I must have complete silence before I can get into that creative place where ideas begin to flow. Does that sound like you? It is important to get in touch with this aspect of yourself, to be aware of what your mind and senses need to help you achieve razor-sharp focus.

The objective when choosing your ideal environment is to put yourself on a one-track path to success. By all means, make notes of the images and thoughts that come to you during these fertile times. I keep a small recorder and a writing pad on my nightstand or in the great room area where I sometimes vegetate when I cannot sleep. Do not trust your short-term memory to recall with clarity the rich details of your thoughts during these times.

Clean up your mental environment. I have a pretty souped-up computer, an Apple G-5. It has tremendous processing capacity and speed and is capable of deploying several highly complex computer programs simultaneously. But for all of its sophistication, even this machine has its limits. When I start stacking functions on top of one another and layering plug-ins and other programs, the machine starts to sweat. While it may not be apparent to new users, I can tell when the CPU is being strained. It is still super fast, mind you, but I can tell the difference.

Your brain reacts to multiple operations just like a CPU. The more you ask it to do, the slower it goes. Eventually, it may even crash. But if you begin removing complex and competing tasks, the faster and more efficiently your brain will operate. So if you want to focus, clean up the clutter in your mind. Close "programs" you are not using currently. This will improve your speed and take away the stress of attending to additional tasks—either consciously or unconsciously—that may be stealing your focus away from the task at hand. This will improve not only your personal efficiency but the quality of your performance as well.

Resources

Years ago, I made a conscious decision never to do anything out of need. That can be a challenging position to take when cash is in short supply. But for the individual who operates from a strong basis of integrity, it can also be the most liberating feeling in the world. What can beat knowing that you stood firm, doing the right thing?

As gallant as that may sound, I also know from experience that one of the greatest focus-busters is lack of finances or other resources. If you are spending all of your time worrying about how you are going to keep the doors open or how you are going to keep a roof over your family's head, how are you ever going to get anything done? We have already gone over some financial principles in Chapter 7. Many excellent resources also exist to help you in this regard. So rather than reinventing the wheel in this section, I would like to share but one key principle: the principle of giving.

In their brilliant work *Just Enough*,[15] authors Laura Nash and Howard Stevenson describe how everyone is struggling with what they call the "Tantalus effect." Tantalus was a mythological creature punished with an eternal, raging thirst. In the same way, many of us seem to be striving constantly for financial success but experiencing only continuous stress and zero contentment. As a way of helping people get off this treadmill, Nash and Stevenson seek to redefine success along nonmonetary lines. Their model of success has four pillars:

1. happiness,

2. achievement,

3. significance, and

4. legacy.

They urge us to set limits on our desires, to determine what is "just enough" for us so we can learn how to live within our means and experience satisfaction regularly along the journey of life instead of it being always just out of reach.

Can you imagine purposely spending less on something than you can afford? Paying off your credit card rather than adding more charges to it? Choosing not to do a certain activity, such as going out for supper once a week, even though you can? That is what achieving "just enough" is all about. There is an interesting offshoot to this approach to life: by setting limits on your needs and desires, eventually you will find yourself with more resources than you need instead of less. So what do you think you should do with this excess?

My suggestion is—brace yourself; this is counterintuitive—that you share it with others. I suggest this not out of a sense of obligation but from henchmen, added this barb: "What they are building—if even a fox climbed up on it, he would break down their wall of stones!" (Nehemiah 4:3 NIV).

To Sanballat and Tobiah's surprise, when Nehemiah and his people reached the halfway stage, suddenly the wall that these feeble people were constructing was looking pretty stable. Predictably, the enemy responded with threats. But Nehemiah and his people kept right on building. Nehemiah 6 records the effect the Jews' actions had on the enemy when they heard the walls were completely restored: "When all our enemies heard about this, all the surrounding nations were afraid and lost their self-confidence, because they realized that this work had been done with the help of our God" (Nehemiah 6:16 NIV).

What better way to utilize the time allotted to us than to act? This is especially true when the alternative to action is negotiation and debate. Planning is vital to success, but you can overindulge in that discipline as well, using it as an escape rather than a precursor to action. There is rarely an equal substitute for the discipline of hard work when it comes to setting an example, winning over detractors, and prevailing despite all opposition.

People like Nehemiah, who are driven with an unswerving purpose, move with high intensity to accomplish their objectives, because they see beyond their actions to the repercussions of their inaction. Nehemiah knew the implications if Jerusalem remained in ruins. He knew how demoralizing a failure would be for this already disheartened people. He also knew that if the city were not rebuilt, the prophecies concerning the promised Messiah would not come to pass. He realized immediately that there was no time for squabbles or ongoing deliberation about whether this course of action or another was right or wrong.

His detractors, however, were not discouraged so easily. With their power base threatened, they implemented every nasty trick they could conceptualize to throw him off course: insults, ridicule, threats, and outright sabotage. Nehemiah refused to be baited by such tactics though. As a result, the wall was completed, and the effect it had on the Jews and their enemies was profound.

The lesson is this: there is no substitute for action. In the time it would have taken Nehemiah to address and deal with each of his detractors' threats and intimidation tactics, he attained his objective on behalf of the God he served. The resentment Nehemiah would have stirred up by responding and engaging his enemies in debate would have wasted time while also fanning the flame of their hatred for him and what he was doing. Moving forward steadily was the only way to overcome his enemies' threats.

Jerusalem was in ruin for nearly one hundred twenty years. Nehemiah fixed the wall in fifty-two days—incredible. This achievement illustrates again the power of people moving with purposeful action, utilizing time as an agent of purpose and maximum benefit rather than wasting it in futile exposition and rhetoric. Nehemiah never wasted time on minutiae. Neither should we.

Nehemiah altered the perspective of everyone: the Jews, the surrounding nations who were skeptical that change could be instituted after so many years, and his enemies, who were threatened by having their power and influence called into question. Nehemiah's prayerful consideration and rapid execution included delegation as well as "real-time" action on his part at each step. He left his powerful position, risked his life and the comfort his royal employer gave him, and traveled in great hardship a tremendous distance, all to illustrate for everyone the seriousness of his intent. Nehemiah took his task seriously, as should we. After all, if something is worth our attention, it should be worth our most committed effort.

Time to Reflect

I have seen something else under the sun: The race is not to the swift or the battle to the strong, nor does food come to the wise or wealth to the brilliant or favor to the learned; but time and chance happen to them all. Moreover, no man knows when his hour will come. (Ecclesiastes 9:11–12 NIV)

When the moment comes to savor your time on earth, will it be something to cherish or regret? In the Scripture passage above, King Solomon reminds us to set aside our awareness of the inequities in life lest they keep us from serving God through the purposeful use of our time. He also reminds us that no one knows when his or her time will come, but we are assured that it will. This reference is often interpreted to mean death—as in, no one knows the hour of his or her death. But, looked at another way, it can also be taken as a reminder that when your "time" comes—that golden moment that will decide your destiny one way or the other—you must seize the opportunity to act. You do not have any guarantee of when this will occur. Therefore, your preparation for that moment must be maintained at all times and at all costs. All of the strategies and principles in this chapter will help you do just that.

CONCLUSION
Final Thoughts

And so . . .

You can wait until a situation forces you to action. You can hang on to inaction for dear life until each finger slips from the bar and you plunge into an uncertain destiny below. You can face that destiny, unplanned, and know it's your default position, know you have forfeited your choice, your destiny now chosen for you by a failure to initiate, a failure to believe in yourself as worthy, qualified, and deserving. You can wait . . . or you can take the initiative and begin to lead.

Now.

Now is always the right moment.

For each person in the limelight, there are thousands who make that limelight occur—working, supporting, and enabling "the Star." As often as not, being a Star is a persona and not much more. Being a Star is not leading; it's utilizing charisma to generate self-serving glory. Being a Star is not a condition that automatically benefits those in supporting roles—those who would be led.

If you believe that if you are not a Star you cannot possibly lead, your mind-set will continue to handicap you. You won't find the initiative to move out of the starting blocks. Can you remember, as Nehemiah did, how it is not necessary to be a king to lead? You can be a humble servant like Nehemiah and still have an impact on those around you. The situational leadership model presented in this book will work if you use it, but will you?

Initiative sets your feet on the path, but then you need to search for your roadmap. Can you find it when you need it? Is it accessible? Each time you recall the content of the map you have drawn for your future, you engrave it a little deeper into your subconscious. You can't become discouraged because other people are able to commit it to memory quickly while you may have to revisit your plan and goals repeatedly to achieve the same focus.

You have your road map, your plan, tucked safely in your hip pocket. You take it out and scan it, remembering the thought and dedication that went into it. You recall how you dreamt for years that your coach would play you. You yearned to be in the starting lineup of the varsity squad. And now? You are the coach. You are the architect of the plan. You are creating your own lineup, and there's your name at the top of the roster, written in your own handwriting. It's your game. There is no more stalling. You are nervous with anticipation and fear. Failure is not an option. But can you succeed? Can you lead?

In your mind, you hear the announcer calling out the lineup. Your name is announced, but you don't hear the crowd. Why? Because there isn't one, and you realize you are alone. You can't depend on the support of fans in this game. Leadership is a solitary pursuit.

It's your game, however, and you call the shots. You can do what you want. That's the beauty as well as the unnerving reality. Suddenly, the outcome of the game rests entirely on your shoulders. This is the time when you realize the moment for action—the result by which your performance will be measured—has arrived. You square your shoulders and walk onto the playing field, replete with Red Zone scenarios, clutching your playbook if only in your mind's eye, palms sweating.

You remind yourself of Nehemiah, who was not only playing to win but playing to live; a man whose enemies routinely set trap upon devious trap for his destruction; a man whose laser focus enabled him to remain on task; a man of humility who took comfort and guidance in his spirituality when his spirit flagged and his plans were jeopardized. Nehemiah strode purposefully onto the field; he entered the fray protected only by his faith. He remained focused and motivated, supercharging his momentum with God's spiritual guidance and supplication. Nehemiah didn't see himself as the star of the game; he recognized glory was for God alone.

If you consider your focus and motivation for action in terms of athletics, you realize that leadership stars are like most athletic stars, natural talent personified. Their focus and motivation come naturally, at a small cost. You recognize how a star may have a lead over the rest of us, but do they really have all the advantages over those who have worked harder and longer to achieve the same results?

Consider a potential advantage you might have—the conditioning achieved through additional hard work, your constant training to persevere, your inability to accept failure no matter how often you falter—the result of struggling to be the best when you are less than the obvious choice. It strengthens you.

When you have failed more often and learned to overcome failure more swiftly without allowing it to break your stride, you gain a powerful advantage over those who rarely have to struggle to achieve the greatest heights.

Skills honed by intensive training are the skills you need as a leader. If you are familiar with struggling, competing, and training to overcome failure, you often find that in seemingly impossible situations, you are in better shape than the stars. But then again, did you have a choice?

Faith and spirituality never lack relevance to your position as leader, because they are the single-most influential factors in terms of staying the course; they supercharge your motivation, your vision, your initiative, and your momentum. Your plan to act means nothing without that motivation, and your motivation will fail to rescue you from pride, greed, lust, and indecision—factors which attempt to undermine you at every twist and turn. To persist through such temptations, malcontented persons, and failures, to withstand the darkness in your own mind, which can cloud your thoughts and undermine your endeavors, you must embrace your faith.

If you still can't shake your doubt about how relevant faith and spirituality are, it can shortchange your aspirations. You need only look around to see evidence of this. Remember, however, that looking at a freeze-frame of a hero's life can bring envy and discontent. Rather, you need to consider the long-term results of a person's life and career. Is his or her entire life one you should emulate?

In the Red Zone, you experience a life situation, a set of circumstances that, taken together, exert tremendous pressure on the system, the team.

When traditional moral convictions and opposing secular norms collide, your leadership strength and capacity are challenged in the extreme. The end result, attainment of the Holy Grail of success, depends on your ability to withstand these temptations and assert your moral convictions. In my experience, embracing and implementing the three core concepts and the seven operating principles I have discussed in this book is the best way to do this.

Core Concepts

Crucible Experiences. Recognize them when they come, use the principles I describe in Chapter 3 to make the most of them, and don't ignore the core values they reveal.

Core Values. Take time to think about what these are for you. Then ask yourself: On what moral or spiritual foundation are my core values based? Do you need to change some of your core values? If so, how?

Visioning. Once your core values are in place, visions should begin to flow naturally. Capture these visions on paper and share them with your team. These will set the agenda for your life.

Operating Principles

Harnessing the Will. The will is where all great causes begin. With your vision in place, use your will to start your own great cause today.

Establishing Traction. Traction is vital to success in every area of life, because until you get your grip, it is impossible to build momentum. Apply the principles in Chapter 7 to make sure the rubber is always meeting the road.

Creating Connectivity. Don't just communicate with your team; *connect* with them. Frame every exchange of information within the context of relationship.

Finding Focus. What is your game plan? Don't allow the flurry of information and experiences that come your way to distract or derail you. Once your vision is in place, stick to it.

Igniting Passion. Discover your passion, develop it, and use it to ignite the flame of passion in others. Become a passion builder, and watch your visions spring to life.

Striking a Balance. Forget about trying to do everything and start doing the right things at the right time. Keep your hands on all the critical points, and remember, properly allocated resources don't always look that way.

Beating the Clock. You can't manage time; you can only manage yourself. Time is the only truly nonrenewable resource. So be sure to make the most of it!

Refusing to recognize when you are entering a Red Zone and responding accordingly can impact your future in ways that are often entirely inconceivable at the time. You must have faith, you must act, and you must do so in accordance with what you know to be right, moral, and true. In the end, that is all you can hope for, all you can achieve. Often, you will find that not only is it enough; it brings you more than you ever dreamed.

ABOUT THE AUTHOR

Spencer Tillman is a sports broadcaster, former NFL player, journalist, businessman, churchgoer, and family man. He has written pieces for the *Wall Street Journal,* the *San Francisco Chronicle,* the *Houston Chronicle,* and others. Tillman was an all-American running back for the University of Oklahoma. He was UPI Player of the Year in the Big Eight Conference in 1982, Most Valuable Player of the 1987 Orange Bowl, and a Heisman Trophy candidate in 1983. In his final year of college, he was drafted by the Houston Oilers. After two seasons, he joined the San Francisco 49ers, where he won a Super Bowl and served as team captain. He returned to Houston in 1992, and played the final two years of his career there. In 1999, Tillman joined CBS Sports for *College Football Today,* where now he also covers NCAA Men's Basketball. Spencer is a devoted husband and father of four daughters.

ACKNOWLEDGMENTS

To suggest this work is by "Spencer Tillman" overstates the truth. There are a dozen or more individuals without whose efforts this book would not be possible. First, to my bride, Rita, who has sacrificed so much to make our marriage work. You perform miracles with our four girls, Alisa, Blair, Mir, and Bailey. I was smitten by your presence some twenty years ago as I streaked through the Red Zone and into the end zone against Ohio State. I was a freshman running back; you were a sophomore pom-pom girl. I will never forget the day I laid eyes on you. Thank you for your unselfish heart and for allowing me the space to write this book. You live out daily what it means to be a godly woman.

Kevin Miller, a.k.a. "K"—the finest writer, editor, and educator on the planet—gently instructed me throughout the creation of this book. I believe our meeting was providential. Where I'd come up short, "K" would be there to add structure and order to my organic style of writing. When done correctly, formula works. You're a pro.

To the Reverend Dr. Greg Headington, who resides in the "circle of three," one of my most important relationships: Our meetings in Washington, D.C., and Florida produced some fine material. You are a treasured mentor and friend.

To brother Kenneth Basile, a passionate teacher of God's truth: Your daily calls lifted my spirits when no one else was cheering.

I owe special thanks to my friends and colleagues Deborah Lake

Monahan, a gifted writer and publicist, and Jim Beckham, my business partner for eleven years and counting.

My sisters Sharon and Bettina were constant sources of inspiration. Sharon, your random "I love you" calls made my day on too many occasions to recall.

My extended haircuts with my barbers, Le Roi and Barbara Houston, netted substantive perspective on many ecumenical topics. The excellent haircuts were a bonus.

To all my high school coaches who helped shape my leadership style, I say thank you. Tommy Thompson, my high school running back coach, showed up at my college graduation ceremonies ringing a cowbell, as promised. Bill Noble showed me what was possible in life beyond the field.

I owe a debt of gratitude to all of my professional coaches as well: Al Lavan, Lynn Stiles, Frank Novak, Ray Sherman, Richard Smith, George Siefert, Mike Holgrem, Kevin Gilbride, Jerry Glanville—"Bula Bula, darling," June Jones, Jack Pardee, and Greg Williams.

And then there are my college coaches: Barry Switzer, who when he told me he loved me seconds before I stepped out onto the turf at Memorial Stadium before the Nebraska game in 1983 changed my life. Coach Merv Johnson recruited me and modeled integrity. Thanks also to Mack Brown, Jim Donan, Scott Hill, and Galen Hall. Each one of you added something to my success on the field.

The fine folk at Thomas Nelson have been a joy to work with. Kyle Olund—I love your spirit. Brian Hampton is a pro's pro. When we first met, someone commented that publishing runs through his veins, and that person could not have been more correct. Your brilliance for identifying what works is a special gift. Jonathan Merkh's support from the outset was evident. Thank you for your leadership. Thanks also to my literary agent, Dave Robie, who brought us all together. Dave, you are a consummate professional.

Special thanks to my high school English teacher Mary Faye McFarlin: God bless you. You saw the potential and encourage me to this day.

To my life-long friends Alvin Sanders, John Blake, Don Smitherman, Al Smith, and Bill and Mary Ann Dickerson: You all have played an important role in keeping me grounded and accountable.

ACKNOWLEDGMENTS

Thanks to all those in the broadcasting arena who have played a role in advancing my network career: Sean McManus, Tony Petitti, Vin DeVito, and Tim Brando. Special thanks also go to Terry Ewert, who gave me my network break. Steve Herz, my broadcasting agent for years, worked hard to open doors. On the local broadcast scene, Al Eschbach gave me my big break in radio. I owe a debt of gratitude to Lee Allan Smith, who opened the door to television broadcasting in 1983. Karim Karim, Bob Barry Sr., and Bob Barry Jr. all showed me the ropes. Steve Ramsey, Steve Wasserman, and Bart Fader hired me at two pivotal stops, KPRC-TV and WABC-TV respectively. To Mike "A" and John Heidke, thanks for the ride at Fox Sports Net.

I've saved the best for last intentionally. To my father Jack Tillman Jr., who left home at age fifteen to help his family make ends meet back in Texas: You're my hero, Daddy. Thank you for persevering during what were difficult times for any African-American male. You remained faithful to La Rue, your wife, for nearly fifty years. Thanks for showing me what commitment looks like and how to provide for my family.

NOTES

1. Michael Lewis, *The New New Thing: A Silicon Valley Story* (New York: Penguin, 2001).

2. http://www.kltv.com/Global/story.asp?S=1460815.

3. http://www.katv.com/news/stories/1103/108378.html.

4. http://www.cdc.gov/niosh/stresswk.html.

5. http://www.bartleby.com/66/25/43525.html.

6. *North Carolina Lawyer*, December 2002.

7. W. H. Murray, "The Scottish Himalayan Expedition" (London: J. M. Dent & Sons, 1951).

8. "The Battle of the Bottoms," *Forbes* (March 24, 1997), 98.

9. Lance Armstrong, *Lance Armstrong Biography*, ESPN Classic, August 1, 2004.

10. John Kao, *Jamming: The Art and Discipline of Business Creativity* (New York: HarperBusiness, 1997), 86.

11. http://www.ltsn-01.ac.uk/about/index_html.

12. Granted, the television still represents a profound degree of separation between the view and the survivor. Just imagine how much more powerful that same experience would be if you were the reporter on the street.

13. http://science.howstuffworks.com/submarine3.htm.

14. http://www.spencerstuart.com.

15. Laura Nash and Howard Stevenson, *Just Enough* (Hoboken, N.J.: Wiley and Sons, 2005).

16. Lisa Keister, "Religion Helps Shape Wealth of Americans," *Journal of Social Forces,* September 2004.

17. Eileen McDargh, "The Art of Balancing an Unequal Life," http://www.eileenmcdargh.com/article_art.html (copyright 2000).